LYONEL FEININGER

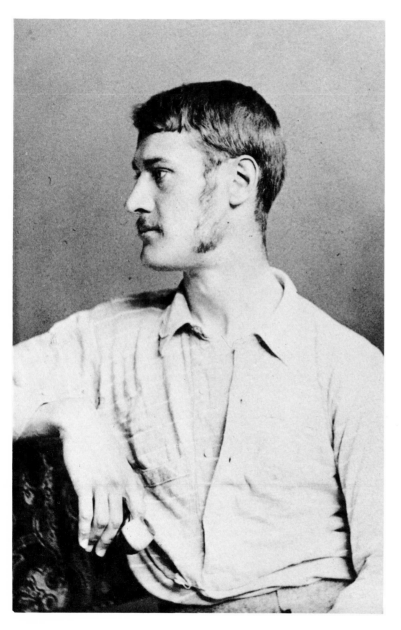

1. Lyonel Feininger, age twenty-three. 1894.

LYONEL FEININGER

caricature & fantasy

BY ERNST SCHEYER
wayne state university

2. *Virtuoso.* Woodcut on yellow paper. Circa 1919.

Wayne State University Press   Detroit, 1964

To Evelyne

CONTENTS

Acknowledgments / *p. 1*

I. *Feininger and America:* Friends, Letters, and Scrapbooks / *p. 5*

II. *Music, Trains, Boats, and Ghosts:* Childhood in America, 1871–87 / *p. 11*

III. *Cartooning and Illustrating:* Study Years in Hamburg, Berlin, Liège, Paris, 1887–1906 / *p. 23*

IV. *From Cartooning to Painting:* Paris, Berlin, 1907–12 / *p. 97*

V. *The Flowering of Fantasy:* Prints, Watercolors, and Paintings of the Later Years; World War I, Bauhaus, and Return to America, 1912–56 / *p. 143*

Appendix I. Selection of Letters from Lyonel Feininger to H. Francis Kortheuer and Alfred Vance Churchill, 1887–1913 / *p. 157*

Appendix II. Letter of H. Francis Kortheuer, March 18, 1959 / *p. 171*

Notes / *p. 177*

Bibliography / *p. 189*

Index / *p. 193*

ILLUSTRATIONS

1. Lyonel Feininger, age twenty-three. 1894.   *frontispiece*
2. *Virtuoso.* Woodcut on yellow paper. Circa 1919.   *title page*
3. *Concert Singer.* Pen drawing. 1893.   *p. 20*
4. Cover illustration for *Fest-Zeitung.* 1888.   *p. 33*
5. *A "Germanized Irishman."* Pen cartoon. 1893.   *p. 36*
6. Letter to H. Francis Kortheuer. 1890.   *p. 37*
7. *Association of the Bearded Sons of Germany (Vereinigung der bärtigen Söhne Germanias).* Pen cartoon. 1893.   *p. 38*
8. Letter to Alfred Vance Churchill. 1890.   *p. 42*
9. Café and houses in Liège. Pen, Chinese white, colored paper. 1890.   *p. 44*
10. Courtyard, Berlin. Watercolor. 1889.   *p. 44*
11. *Roofs in Snow (Dächer im Schnee).* Two-color illustration for *Narrenschiff.* 1898.   *p. 50*
12. Art student and instructor. Pen cartoon. 1889.   *p. 50*
13. *Dead-eye and lea-board with fastenings.* Pen and watercolor. 1892.   *p. 52*
14. Illustration for Brete Harte's "A Ship of '49." Pen and watercolor. 1890.   *p. 52*
15. Pencil tracing of illustration for *Harper's Young People.* 1894.   *p. 61*
16. *Old Woman with Child.* Pen illustration intended for *Harper's Young People.* 1894.   *p. 61*
17. *Ye Learned Apothecary.* Pencil, watercolor, opaque white. 1901.   *p. 62*
18. Feininger with brigantine. 1894.   *p. 65*
19. *Fame (Der Ruhm).* Panel cartoon for *Ulk.* Circa 1898.   *p. 71*
20. *Editorial Staff and Prosecuting Attorney (Redaktion und Staatsanwalt).* Pen cartoon for *Narrenschiff.* 1898.   *p. 73*
21. Carousing fraternity-student. Pen cartoon for *Ulk.* 1895.   *p. 73*

22. *How to Make Pianos Harmless (Unschädlichmachung der Klaviere)*. Color cartoon for *Ulk*. Circa 1895. p. 74

23. *The Electric Horse (Das elektrische Pferd)*. Color cartoon for *Ulk*. Circa 1894. p. 75

24. Navigation problems of air-borne canal traffic. Color cartoon for *Ulk*. Circa 1896. p. 75

25. "Deutschmeer, D-e-u-t-schmeer, ü-ü-ber Alles!" leo feininger. *Ulk Marinier*. Pen cartoon for *Ulk*. 1896. p. 76

26. Details of old ships traced from etchings. 1894. p. 76

27. *Marine*. Etching. 1911. p. 78

28. *Conservative Disunity (Konservative Veruneinigung)*. Cover illustration for *Ulk*. 1897. p. 80

29. *Execution*. Cover illustration for *Lustige Blätter*. Circa 1902. p. 82

30. Cover illustration for *Narrenschiff*. 1898. p. 87

31. *"Off with the Pigtail" ("Zopf ab")*. Book jacket illustration. Circa 1900. p. 87

32. *Blood Rain (Der Blutregen)*. Color cartoon for *Ulk*. 1901. p. 88

33. *Grandpa at the Wheel (Grosspapa auf dem Rad)*. Pen cartoon for *Narrenrad*. Circa 1898. p. 90

34. *In the Bicycle Clinic (In der Radfahr-Klinik)*. Pen cartoon for *Ulk*. 1897. p. 91

35. *Easter Tour of the "Greased Chain" Bicycle Club (Ostertour des Radler-Klub "Geschmierte Kette")*. Color cartoon for *Narrenschiff*. Circa 1898. p. 92

36. *The Prudent Schemer (Le Prévoyant Fraudeur)*. Color cartoon for *Le Témoin*. 1907. p. 105

37. *Moloch à Paris*. Color cartoon for *Le Témoin*. 1906. p. 105

38. *The Three Aunts (Die drei Muhmen)*. Illustration from *Norwegische Volksmärchen*. 1908. p. 110

39. First sketches for "The Kin-der-Kids." Pen, crayon, watercolor. 1906 (date on sketch incorrect). p. 114

40. *"The Kin-der-Kids portrait gallery."* Color cartoon series for the *Chicago Sunday Tribune*. Entire series copyrighted 1906. p. 115

41. "The Kin-der-Kids." *Piemouth Is Rescued by Kind-Hearted Pat*. p. 117

42. "The Kin-der-Kids." *Narrow Escape from Aunty Jim-Jam*. p. 118

43. "Wee Willie Winkie's World." Color cartoon series for the *Chicago Sunday Tribune.* Nov. 25, 1906.   *p. 119*

44. "Wee Willie Winkie's World." Dec. 2, 1906.   *p. 121*

45. Village street, near Heringsdorf. Crayon sketch. 1909.   *p. 135*

46. Strollers on Heringsdorf beach. Crayon sketch. 1911.   *p. 136*

47. Thuringian village scene. Crayon sketch. 1913.   *p. 138*

48. *Lokomotive.* Drypoint. 1906.   *p. 144*

49. Pen and watercolor letterheads. 1951.

    a) *Ill-Tempered Clavier.*   *p. 148*

    b) *"Tristesse," "Lamentation," "Wehklage."*   *p. 148*

    c) *Choir-rehearsal.*   *p. 148*

50. Feininger with bicycle. 1894.   *p. 161*

ACKNOWLEDGMENTS

The manuscript for this book has undergone many changes. It was begun as an introduction to letters written by Lyonel Feininger to Alfred Vance Churchill and to the original sketches and clippings pasted by this friend of his Berlin student years into a scrapbook. These were among the treasures of the Archives of American Art in Detroit, Michigan. To their founder and director, Edgar P. Richardson, and former Archivist Miriam Lucker Lesley go my sincerest thanks for letting me use these substantially unpublished documents.

After Hans Hess, Curator of the Art Gallery of the City of York, England, had visited Detroit in connection with the preparation of his comprehensive book on Lyonel Feininger, an exchange of information began from which I benefited vastly. Mr. Hess also introduced me to Mrs. Julia Feininger of New York. The artist's widow and her son Theodore Lux Feininger of Cambridge, Mass., were kind enough to grant me permission to publish those letters from Lyonel Feininger to his friend, Alfred Vance Churchill, which dealt with Feininger's artistic development as a cartoonist, illustrator, and painter. Their consent and advice are here gratefully acknowledged.

Correspondence with Mr. and Mrs. Dayrell Kortheuer of Charlotte, North Carolina, directed me to still another set of postcards and letters by Lyonel Feininger, many of them illustrated by original sketches which were carefully preserved by their father, the late H. Francis Kortheuer of Daytona Beach, Florida. These letters shed light on the artist's youth in America. Before his death, H. Francis Kortheuer gave permission to publish a selection of these letters and furnished a brief record of his relationship with

Feininger which will be found in the Appendix. At the time of the sale of the Kortheuer summer house in Lime Rock, Connecticut, a second scrapbook, long believed lost, was rediscovered by the heirs. It contained a collection of original cartoons, clippings, and tracings of drawings done for American and German humor magazines still larger than that made by Churchill. The greater number of illustrations in this book derive from these two scrapbooks. For the excellent reproductions of these illustrations I am indebted to Joseph Klima of the Detroit Institute of Arts.

The persons contacted by mail and in person to explain certain points in Feininger's letters are too numerous to acknowledge here. To all of them my thanks are extended. Frau Margarete Moll of Düsseldorf, sculptor and painter, a Matisse pupil and my revered friend, deserves special mention for her delightful letter on meeting the Feiningers in Paris in 1906 in the "Circle of the Café du Dôme."

To Mrs. Mary M. Churchill of Northampton, Mass., the widow of Alfred Vance Churchill, I owe considerable information on the life of her late husband.

Another friend of Feininger's Berlin student years, Fred Werner, late of Lindfield, N.S.W., Australia, a well-known retired organist, contributed valuable details and sent the originals of the illustrations to Bret Harte's short story "A Ship of 49," as well as some illustrations for Dante's *Inferno* done by Feininger for him, which he had taken to his native Australia.

Meanwhile, the material of a study on the "Early Feininger" grew in such an encouraging way that I changed the character of the planned publication from an "Introduction to Letters" to a study on "The Development of Lyonel Feininger from Cartoonist to Painter." Since substantial parts of the letters are now incorporated into the text, only four letters from the two complete sets have been printed in the appendix—these four seemed most interesting from the standpoint of the growth of Feininger's character and art. In all of these letters, certain peculiarities and mistakes in English spelling have been retained, as well as the occasional use of German words and phrases, since they lend a distinct flavor and charm to Feininger's writing style. Also, whenever it seemed appropriate or useful, I have given the English translations of the titles for German books, magazines, illustrations, paintings, and cartoons as they first appear in the letters or in the text.

The considerable rewriting of the text made new use of the German edition of Hans Hess's book *Lyonel Feininger,* published in 1959 by W. Kohlhammer, Stuttgart. All quotations from Hess's book have been translated by me from the German edition. The "Oeuvre Catalogue" (quoted in my text as such) compiled by Mrs. Julia Feininger for Hess's publication was of especial help in this phase of the book.

The Lyonel Feininger Memorial Exhibition 1959–61 held in several museums in this country and Germany (which I studied at The Cleveland Museum and at the Hamburg Kunsthalle) was a great inspiration. Added to the exhibition of paintings, water-colors and drawings at Cleveland, and not shown at the other places to which the show travelled, was a collection of Feininger's graphic work and the charming letterheads in pen and watercolor from the correspondence of Lyonel Feininger to his son, the Reverend Father Laurence Feininger of Trent, Italy. To him go my thanks for publication rights and also to the Associate Curator of Prints at the Cleveland Museum, Miss Leona E. Prasse, for having expertly and lovingly brought together this delightful bonus to the Memorial Exhibit. Miss Prasse is compiling a catalogue of Feininger's graphic work which is eagerly awaited by all friends of the artist. Meanwhile, she was so generous as to assist me with information and photographs from her domain of specialization.

Dr. Alan Fern, curator of prints and photographs at the Library of Congress, Washington, D.C., assisted me in securing photographs of the comic strips done by Feininger for *The Chicago Sunday Tribune.* These strips have not been previously reproduced. To Dr. Fern and the Library of Congress staff go my thanks for granting me publication rights to this material.

Among my other friends I am most gratefully indebted to

Professor Margaret Sterne of the History Department of Wayne State University, who wrote for me an essay on German Foreign and Interior policy for the years between 1897–1907, the time during which Feininger worked for *Ulk* (The Sunday Supplement of the *Berliner Tageblatt*). Originally intended to appear in the appendix, its most valuable information has now been incorporated into the text.

Finally, my most heartfelt thanks are to be expressed to the members of the Wayne State University Press, to its director, my cherished colleague for over a quarter of a century, Dr. Harold A. Basilius, and to Richard Kinney, the art director, for the design. Of the people who have helped in editing the manuscript, my most sincere thanks go to Richard Dey, who gave the manuscript its final shape and whose interest in the field of caricature and especially in that of the American cartoon has enriched this book. My thanks also goes to Mrs. Judith Parker for preparation of the Index.

E. S.
Detroit, Michigan, 1964

FEININGER AND AMERICA

Friends, Letters and Scrapbooks

Lyonel[1] Feininger's art belongs both to Germany and the United States. Recognized as one of the leaders of modern German art during the years he was connected with the "Bauhaus," he has emerged since his death in New York in 1956 as an artist whose life and work reflect the forces of our age rather than those of any specific "ism" such as cubism or expressionism.

Second only to Whistler in importance among America's artist-expatriates, this native New Yorker is certainly more deserving of the term "modern" both in the sense of time and space than many later, more widely publicized and sensational painters.

Feininger's art reflects his fascination with the world of modern technology. Trains, boats, bicycles, typewriters and cameras were his passionate interests. The automobile, however, rarely appears in his repertoire of mechanical objects, no doubt because it had not been in wide use until some time after the youthful Feininger had left America.

From Feininger's earliest years his interest in moving mechanisms was inseparably linked with life in a big city. His sensitive eye and fertile imagination were irresistibly attracted to the ceaselessly expanding metropolis, with its rapid tempo, multi-storied architecture, elevated railroads, and viaducts. New York, Hamburg, Berlin, Paris, and towards the end of his life New York again —each city in turn exerted a profound influence on his art and thought. Although he also stayed in small provincial towns such as Weimar and Dessau, and vacationed in the country and at the seashore whenever he could because of his love of rural peace and the majesty of the sea, it was the metropolitan milieu that most decisively formed Feininger's character and art.

Moving mechanisms and the big city found their earliest artistic expression in his work not only in technologically exact renderings of real and imaginary cities, bridges, viaducts, trains and boats, but also in caricatures and cartoons. Cartooning is a characteristically American art activity which rapidly became a powerful form of pictorial journalism during Feininger's early years. It now ranks prominently among the popular arts and is of increasing interest to the art historian as well as the sociologist. The main root of Feininger's cartoons and caricatures was his abounding sense of fantasy. Through his drawings he exorcised the ghosts and demons he saw as a child.

From his early childhood, music was an essential part of Feininger's daily life. His parents were both gifted and well-known musicians, and it was through their enthusiasm and influence that music became both a duty and a delight for the boy. Feininger gradually began to sense a spiritual, religious power in music that transcended the purely sensuous. It was this spiritual element that formed the unifying force in his uniquely personal style, transforming organized sound into an architecture of color, light, and space. Cartooning eventually began to prove inadequate as an outlet for Feininger's burgeoning lyrical and architectural sensibilities; he moved on to etching, lithography, woodcuts, and then to watercolor and painting, mediums in which his true genius found its fullest expression.

The four major elements that formed Feininger's creative genius were all rooted in his American childhood and found expression at an early age: his feeling for city life, his interest in technology, his high-strung sensitivity, and his abiding interest in music. Although he was trained for a career in music from an early age, Feininger's primary artistic expression seems to have been visual rather than auditory, and by the age of sixteen these forces led him to concentrate on the graphic arts.

From the hour of Feininger's birth onward, the conditions for his developing an original style were both complicated and enriched by the fact that he was born in New York into a German-

American family and milieu. It is because of this and the fact that he spent fifty of his most creative years in Germany that the artist is registered in the history of German as well as American modern art, and in the former earlier than in the latter. Efforts to reclaim Feininger for America were made in the country of his birth only after his return to New York in 1937. There remains however the indisputable fact that Feininger's reputation was made in Germany and rested on the achievements of his middle years.

Lately, both German and American art historians and critics have increasingly expressed the opinion that Feininger's "old age style" after his return to America constitutes his most spiritual phase and the fruition of his art and life.

Since this is also the period in which his fantasy had reached its sublime heights, tracing the gradual process of transformation from caricature to "pure fantasy"—an expression Feininger loved to use in the letters to the two American friends of his youth—seems a worthwhile effort.

Feininger's life and art may be viewed, then, as a triptych with a wide centerpiece and two smaller wings. The wing to the left would represent his American childhood: the sixteen years from 1871 to 1887. The wing to the right would represent the final period of his life, spent again in America: the eighteen-and-a-half years from 1937 to 1956. The middle portion, the fifty years from 1887 to 1937 that spanned his youth and maturity, belong to Europe, and, more specifically, to Germany.

The importance of this middle period in duration and fame does not alter the fact that Feininger's personal style during these European years remained conditioned by his American past, where the formative elements of his art—technology, music and fantasy—first appeared. This was felt strongly by his German friends and critics and was always acknowledged by Feininger himself. As a young man in Germany, he was always quite proud of his characteristically American appearance (see frontispiece). The most significant indication of his American affinities, however, was the fact that he kept his American citizenship throughout his fifty years of residence in Germany, even though this was often inconvenient and even dangerous, especially after the United States had joined forces with the Allies during World War I, at which time Feininger suffered many privations and a kind of half-internment.

Feininger's letters offer the greatest testament to his struggles as an artist, especially those in which he tried to explain himself to the people closest to him. In a letter of 1917 he wrote: "My paintings alone can prove that I was justified to create in my peculiar way. After my death, when, maybe, my written statements will be collected, they might help to explain further my work as a painter."

Certainly the most important of Feininger's letters are those to his wife Julia and to his three sons, Andreas, Theodore Lux, and Laurence, but since these communications are to be published in the near future, this book has made use mainly of those letters written to two friends of his youth and young manhood: H. Francis Kortheuer and Alfred Vance Churchill. Since both men were Americans, the correspondence was carried on in English, amusingly interspersed at times with German and French.

During the winter of 1888–89, when he was seventeen, Feininger met Alfred Vance Churchill in Berlin while both young men were students at the Königliche Akademie der Bildenden Künste. Churchill was seven years older than Feininger, had already received a bachelor's degree from Oberlin College, and was much more advanced than his friend in the field of watercolor landscapes. After a similar beginning, the life, interests, and art of the two developed in different directions. During his stays in Paris, Churchill had become an admirer of the impressionists, an enthusiasm Feininger did not share. However, Churchill's other enthusiasms for landscapes, watercolor, and the paintings of J. M. W. Turner did exert a considerable influence on Feininger, an influence clearly revealed in his letters and in a comparison of the watercolors (which Churchill pasted carefully into his scrapbook) that the two art students painted during 1889 and 1890.[2]

Born in Oberlin, Ohio, on August 14, 1864, Churchill was the son of a distinguished professor of physics, astronomy and sacred music at the local college. Oberlin, founded only thirty-two years before Churchill's birth, was rapidly becoming one of the Midwest's leading colleges.[3] Churchill entered Oberlin in 1881, concentrating on the liberal arts and music until he was awarded his bachelor's degree in 1887. He then decided to become a painter in earnest, and since Oberlin could not offer adequate instruction he left for Europe to study art and art history, first at the academies of Berlin and Leipzig (1887–90), and then at a number of Parisian art schools and L'Académie Julian (1890).

Churchill married Marie Marshall, a concert singer, during a visit to Berlin in 1890, and returned to America with her in the following year. During the next few years he held teaching posts in the art departments of several leading schools[4] and received his master's degree from Oberlin in 1896. Eight years later he left again for Paris and studied at the Sorbonne from 1904 to 1906. Upon his return to America later in 1906, he accepted a post at Smith College as professor of the History and Interpretation of Art. Churchill eventually became the director of the college Museum of Art and developed one of the finest collections of nineteenth-century French art in this country.[5] During these later years he devoted himself increasingly to the study of art history and aesthetics, interests which had absorbed him since his first teaching days in the United States. He died in Northampton, Massachusetts, on December 29, 1949.

While artistic problems stand in the forefront of the subjects treated by Feininger in his correspondence with Churchill, nostalgic memories of a common childhood in New York and the countryside of New Jersey dominate the letters he exchanged with H. Francis Kortheuer, his childhood friend. Kortheuer, like Feininger, was the son of a musician and came from a German-American background. They shared the problems and advantages of an education in two cultures, and although they were separated for many years, their friendship lasted to the end of Feininger's life.

(For further details, refer to Mr. Kortheuer's letter to the author in the Appendix.)

When Feininger and Kortheuer were boys they engaged in many friendly competitions, drawing, carving and building model trains and boats, making fanciful maps of cities, and collecting stamps. After planning to study architecture, Kortheuer became a highly successful development engineer and came to represent to Feininger the world of technology that he so admired. Once, in a mood of depression, Feininger came to doubt his artistic vocation, and in a letter to Kortheuer in 1898 he expressed his envy of his engineer friend's success and security. Since the correspondence with Kortheuer often concerns America, these letters are an especially rich source of information about Feininger's relationship to his native land.

If Feininger's belief that the most incisive and lasting impressions which nourished his art were received during his childhood is correct, then one can find in these letters the key to that mysterious blend of ingredients from which that phenomenon called individual style is crystallized.

MUSIC, TRAINS, BOATS, AND GHOSTS

Childhood in America, 1871–87

In the turbulent period following the Civil War, the United States changed rapidly from a largely undeveloped land to a highly industrialized and urbanized nation. The magic wand of mechanization which brought about this transformation touched the lives of all who lived in the big cities of the time. Lyonel Feininger, born in the New York of 1871, was particularly sensitive to that touch. Although he remained under the spell of the new forms of technology which arose during his boyhood for the rest of his life, Feininger's heritage of German culture and his parents' devotion to music were equally strong influences contributing to the synthesis of Feininger's art.

When Lyonel's father, Karl Friedrich Wilhelm Feininger, was four years old, his parents brought him to America. This was in the aftermath of the abortive German democratic revolution of 1848, when many freedom-loving Germans—among them Carl Schurz—came to the New World. Both Karl and his father, Alois Adolph Michael Feininger, were born in Durlach, a small residential town in Baden where the elder Feininger owned a china shop. Karl's mother Lena, born Brennioni, was a descendant of a Venetian family which like many others had come to the small courts of southern Germany during the eighteenth century. The Feiningers' new home was Charleston, South Carolina.

When he was about fourteen years old, Karl returned to Germany to study violin at the famous Leipzig Conservatory, founded twenty years before by Felix Mendelssohn and especially popular with American music students. According to a story told in the family, Karl was a roommate and close friend of August D. F. von Wilhelmi (1845–1908) who later became an internationally famous violinist. (It is known that both young musicians studied under the same teachers at the conservatory.) At the outbreak of the Civil War, when he was only sixteen, Karl returned to his family in America and enlisted—it is said—in the bugle corps of the Confederate Army.

When the war ended Karl's father retired to Columbia, South Carolina. Karl himself settled in New York, where he married Elisabeth Cecilia Lutz, a pianist, organist, and singer, and the daughter of a captain in the Union Army. She had been born in Elizabeth, New Jersey in 1848, and like her husband was of mixed ancestry; her mother's family had come from Arles in southern France. The young couple's first home was at 85 St. Mark's Place in old Manhattan, and it was there that their son Lyonel spent his early childhood.[1]

After their marriage, the Feiningers frequently performed together in recitals. Their first joint concert took place on December 28, 1870 and was followed by extensive tours. They performed in the United States, France, and South America, where they played for the Emperor of Brazil. Although the two artists seemed to have much in common—their interest in music, their German and Latin ancestry, and their Catholic religion—they were incompatible, and their marriage eventually ended in separation.

It is unfortunate that Karl Feininger never wrote his memoirs, since as a music teacher, violinist and composer, he was closely associated with the development of musical life in New York City. He was a well-known figure in that group of German-American musicians[2]—which included Leopold Damrosch and his son Walter —who made outstanding contributions to the growth of vocal and instrumental music in the city during the 1870's and 1880's.

Karl Feininger's greatest fame was as a violin virtuoso who "held large audiences" in New York as late as 1917.[3] His name appears in the *Annals of the New York Stage*[4] for the first time in 1868, when he gave a recital with his sister Gabrielle; she was called a *prima donna assoluta* and Karl was likened to Paganini. Karl performed alone, with his wife, or in chamber music groups in the Apollo Hall, Chickering Hall, Steinway Hall, Metropolitan Concert Hall, and several New York churches.

As a composer he was less successful. His songs were occasionally played in German-American circles, and *Fourteen Lieder to Victor von Scheffel's "Trompeter von Säckingen"* were published in Leipzig. Some of his other compositions are preserved in the Library of Congress.

Music ruled the Feininger household. The oft-repeated family story that Karl played chamber music in his home while his son Lyonel was being born in the next room is perhaps apocryphal. But Lyonel himself gives an authentic description of this government of music and its lasting influence on him in a letter he wrote in 1905:

I remember so well: When I was a very small boy, four or five years old, in New York, we lived in a three-story house all by ourselves: I used to sit in the dusk in the big dining room in the basement. The large stove gave heat also to the music room above. The register of the stove was open for me so that I might hear the better—and there I was—perfectly entranced, while my parents were playing, my father the violin, my mother accompanying him on the piano, music by Bach, Beethoven, Mendelssohn, Schumann, Schubert. Waves of delight went through me—I believe nobody ever had an idea what was happening within me: later anyhow my father didn't consider me to be deeply musical. But maybe my inclination for technical constructions, which then had the upper-hand, was not very favorably looked upon by my father, I tinkered too much for his taste—he didn't like it, that I was able to drive pins so straightly into the wooden models which I was building all the time—miniature ships, locomotives and such—he seemed to think that this precluded all feeling for art.[5]

Even though most of his formative years were spent in America, Karl Feininger must have been quite the old-school German, both as a musician and as a father. Since his spiritual home was the pre-industrial Germany of poetry, music and philosophy, he was very much concerned with the dignity and rank of his calling. He supervised young Lyonel's daily violin practice, which sometimes lasted six hours, and had the boy draw the staves for his compositions.

Lyonel, whose serious study of music had started when he was nine, began to appear in concerts three years later. But, as his letter shows, music was not his only love. His preoccupation with locomotives and ships, his tinkering and model-building—regarded by his father as adverse to "all feeling for art"—absorbed him equally. Music and mechanisms—whose union his father deplored—were elements which Lyonel later blended in his art.

For a boy growing up in New York in the seventies and eighties, the phenomenal spread of the city, brought about by the progress of industrialism, mechanization and transportation, must have proved fascinating and irresistible. It was only a short walk from the Feiningers' three-story house on Fifty-third Street to Grand Central Station, the new metal-and-glass hall built by Commodore Vanderbilt's New York Central in 1871. Lyonel would stand on the footbridges that spanned the Fourth Avenue tracks and watch the locomotives and the endless perspective of silvery rails. From this vantage point he could see the trains race along the ravine of Fourth Avenue and gradually emerge from darkness to light. The locomotives had diamond smokestacks and jutting cowcatchers; their driving wheels were painted a bright vermilion, while "the boiler and the fancy steam domes were of polished brass."[6] The excitement and lyricism that permeate Feininger's portraits of locomotives are evocative of Whitman's lines from *To a Locomotive in Winter:*

Thy black cylindric body, golden brass and silvery steel,
Thy ponderous side-bars, parallel and connecting rods, gyrating,
    shuttling at thy sides,
Thy metrical, now swelling pant and roar, now tapering in the
    distance,
Thy great protruding head-light fix'd in front,

. . . .

Type of the modern—emblem of motion and power—pulse of the
    continent . . .

Images of bridges, viaducts, ravines and locomotives impressed Feininger so vividly that they never left him. Always depicted in the style and manner of the seventies, they became root symbols in his art.

The elevated on Second Avenue was also built in the late seventies. After more than sixty years, Feininger's words still convey his excitement over that spectacular achievement in modern metal construction:

In the late seventies, I saw the Second Avenue "L" built . . . the heavy cast iron pedestals brought from somewhere uptown on drays . . . the girders and finally the structure extending as far as the eye could reach, downtown-ward in a terrific row.[7]

That marvel of engineering and design, the Brooklyn Bridge, kept all New York enthralled during the thirteen years of its construction from 1870 to 1883. It must have been an object of especial pride to the city's German immigrant families, since it was the work of the German-American engineer John A. Roebling and his son Washington. Feininger does not mention the bridge in his letters, but as a boy he collected books, articles, and pictures about the structure and its creators. His work ends with a vision of the bridge: in 1953 he painted a water color (collection of Mrs. Julia Feininger) in which its Gothic structure stands out against a yellow ground. His last unfinished oils also deal with the same subject.

The skeleton of the bridge loomed in the distance when Lyonel took his daily walks along the East River, but it seems that the hundreds of boats and ships that passed under it had more interest for him at that time.

It was the time of transition from sailboat to steamer, and brigs, schooners, sloops, sidewheelers and paddle steamboats sailed or steamed by at all times. He knew them all as well as a youngster of today knows the different makes of cars. Three retired sea-captains[8] taught him how to build model yachts, and he sailed them on a pond in Central Park. He followed the yacht races with the eye of an expert. The sailboat, a lasting interest to be shared later with his sons, became another root image in his art.

Toward the end of the seventies came the bicycle craze. Bike clubs sprang up everywhere, and the streets were filled with cyclists perched on vehicles with high front wheels, called Draisinen in Germany, after their inventor, Baron Karl Drais von Sauerbronn.[9] In 1908 he made a drawing of such cyclists in Biedermeier costume, called *Draisinenfahrer*. They also appear in such early paintings as *Draisinenfahrer* (1910).[10] Feininger never saw an automobile before he went to Europe. He depicted it occasionally in his caricatures for German magazines around 1903 and in the pen and ink drawing of 1908, *Auto Champions*.

Just as he had missed the evolution of the car in America, Feininger also missed the early development of the skyscraper. In the seventies and eighties, New York had a number of "high houses," since inventions like the hydraulic elevator (1857) permitted a height of eighteen to twenty stories. But the metal frame skyscraper emerged in Minneapolis—with the theoretical work of Leroy S. Buffington—and in Chicago, where William Le Baron Jenney's Home Insurance Company Building (1883–85) was America's first true skyscraper. When Feininger left New York in 1887, downtown Manhattan did not yet offer the gigantic spectacle which greeted him almost fifty years later on his return. After his homecoming, the sight of these buildings acted as new inspirations, but in his American youth the image of the "high house" as a symbol of man's highest aspirations was developed from church and tower. And they spoke to him most purely in the country. Mill and cemetery, the other "arch-images" which Feininger mentions in his letters to Adolph Knoblauch,[11] are also rooted in a rural setting.

During one of his parents' long absences, the boy and his two younger sisters, Helen and Elsa, stayed with a farm family in Sharon, Connecticut. There Lyonel came to know the New England winter and discovered the pleasures of winter sports. He remembered "the snow, the sleighing, the cold . . . a favorite stove with Gothic doors—we called it Cathedral—showing the flames like a living thing. . . . I would watch lying before it on the floor.

The family of the farmer sat behind us and told ghost stories."[12]

This childhood memory has the flavor of the naïve and intimate representations of winter pleasures found in Currier and Ives prints.[13] Feininger must have seen these colorful pictures of simple country life in the New England winter, as he undoubtedly saw the prints of locomotives, steamers, and fire engines published by the New York firm. However, similarities between these popular prints and later works by Feininger can be sensed rather than indicated, and depend in the main on similar American subject matter.

Lyonel Feininger's impressions of America were those of a boy growing up in a big city who only occasionally enjoyed the pleasures of travel and countryside. But because his journeys away from the city were rare and unusual, they remained so vividly engraved in his memory that long afterward he would talk about them and incorporate them into his art. On many occasions he told his son Lux of the months he had spent at his grandfather's home in South Carolina. This sole visit to the South, the region where his family had originally settled, occurred when Lyonel was twelve years old and recuperating from a serious illness. Lux Feininger tells of these talks in his article "Two Painters":

Family matters were, in these tales, always touched upon with the greatest forbearance (for which it seems there was some need), but the theme which occurred with the greatest clarity was of a visual, and I should like to say symbolic nature . . . the remembered image of dark figures silhouetted against the sky, with a sheet of calm water reflecting at their feet. Investigation of the phenomenon reveals the fact that these figures were some idle negroes fishing in a canal; but it does not require too bold a flight of fancy to see the relationship in the recurrence of this theme of enigmatic figures (with details suppressed) standing on a bank with fishing poles in their hands, silhouetted against the sky. This is the most typical of all the Feininger motifs, his love for architecture notwithstanding.[14]

Lyonel also took trips with his father. In 1883 they traveled on the St. Lawrence River, and two years later they visited Niagara

Falls. A photograph taken during this trip shows Karl and Lyonel Feininger and an unidentified man wearing a top hat, with the Falls and the bridge in the background.[15]

The childhood landscapes that made the deepest impression on Feininger, however, were provided by the gentle hills of Connecticut rolling toward the evening, the broad valleys, isolated farmhouses and sheds, and huge old trees that almost hid the steeple of the village church. After his mother and sisters left for Germany in 1887, Lyonel again lived for a short time in the country. He roomed in Plainfield, New Jersey, about twenty-five miles from New York City, while working as a messenger boy in the Wall Street brokerage firm of one of his father's friends. For the princely salary of seven dollars a week he became a daily commuter at the age of fifteen, scuttling between the New Jersey countryside and lower Manhattan with its swarming cabs and throngs of serious gentlemen in black clothes and top hats. On one of his commuting trips he was nearly killed in a railroad accident, which he describes vividly in words and drawings in a letter to Kortheuer.[16] But these letters from Plainfield tell also of the great fun he had on fishing trips, boating expeditions, and picnics at Lake George in New York State. A typical American scene is sensitively described in this letter of July 17, 1887:

. . . When you were here, do you remember that hall where the revivalist was preaching, on the corner near our house and we stopped outside? Well, service, is being held there and they are all singing hymns, which sound very pleasant on the night air.

The impressions Lyonel formed from works of art seen at home are only partly known, but they cannot have been numerous. He remembered that as a small boy he had seen a big book with steel engravings by Turner—"a classical work."[17] He once told of how he had been taken to the Metropolitan Museum when he was six or seven: ". . . of all the paintings I saw the only ones to make a deep impression on me were from a very early period; they represented Gothic architecture with figures, bright and beautiful in color and clearly silhouetted. For many years I carried the recollection of these pictures with me. It seems to me they influenced my development as a painter."[18]

Conventional religion and the supernatural also had considerable influence on Feininger's development as man and artist. Both sprang from the same root—compounded of loneliness, melancholy, fear and yearning. Religious experiences and ghostly visions were mingled from childhood and became purified as Feininger matured, culminating in the religious glorification of light, space and infinity in his art.

In the farmhouse in Sharon he met simple pious folk and "saw the Bible for the first time."[19] In his own words, he remained "ever since fundamentally religious." The countryside offered divine protection and the companionship of plain, God-fearing people, while the big city often frightened the boy frequently left there by his parents to fend for himself. A painting of 1916, *The Deserted Child*,[20] is unique in Feininger's work. It shows a boy abandoned and desolately huddled on the ground while several tall figures, their backs turned to him, walk off in different directions. It certainly has biographical significance. In moments of loneliness "he imagined faces lurking in the moving shadows" under the elevated and was haunted by "ghost-like apparitions and forms not of this world."[21]

On one hot summer day, while his parents were on tour, Lyonel was "left behind with friends who had a florist shop on Third Avenue," where he was overwhelmed by the scent of tuberoses in funeral wreaths. As he sat in the open doorway he "watched the trains go by overhead, and all the white faces in the windows seemed to him to be ghosts and he began to draw ghosts."[22] A childhood experience which Feininger related to Barr[23] also led to drawing ghosts. "Looking across the East River to Blackwell's Island" he saw "stripe-suited prisoners walking in lock step. This made a wretched impression on me—in consequence I took to drawing ghosts for a while and this may have laid the foundation for my later works, fantastic figures and caricatures."

3. *Concert Singer*. Pen drawing. 1893.

In a fit of melancholy when he "was just unhappy and had to work extra hard at the office" while "Papa and Mama were not here," as he complains in a letter to Kortheuer from Plainfield, August 5, 1885, he added to the words a cartoon of a *Monument to Two Friends.* It shows two little men clasping hands on a stone pedestal; at the right are two graves, one with the inscription "Leo F. died 1974," the other with "Frank K. died 1974. The pedestal is decorated with boats and railroads and a note at the bottom reads: "The pedestal costs $200,000."

The *Concerts* which the two friends drew are savage and grotesque rather than humorous, no doubt reflecting a boyish resentment against the domination of their musician fathers—one of these drawings depicts an orchestra with the violinists holding their instruments upside down. A postcard from Berlin, August 13, 1888, shows the caricature of a violinist done in the manner of Wilhelm Busch. Five years later Feininger mailed Churchill a caricature of a concert singer, possibly representing his mother (fig. 3).

To the psychologist, such a rebellion against parental authority seems normal. It is all the more understandable in the case of two boys who were often derided by their elders for occupying themselves with drawing, painting, carving trains and boats, playing with blocks and coloring maps. The parents considered these activities childish play, and Lyonel was often forbidden to see his friend because of their mutual interests, which he describes in words and a cartoon in a letter to Kortheuer from Plainfield, July 17, 1887:

I am just this minute, 7:43 P.M. Sunday night, gaslit, seated by the light at the round table surrounded by papers innumerable, water, water colors, ink, polygraf, pencils, ruler, several books and your letter. . . . I write fine and small now and think it looks better, or more cosey.

The boys were dreamers and engineer-scientists, builders of railroads and boats, planners of cities and networks of elevated

20

railroads. They possessed not only an extraordinarily precocious knowledge of engineering science, but a meticulous technique in rendering their ideas on paper, abilities exhibited in the charming drawings of locomotives, railroad cars, and boats, and in maps of cities and railroads that fill their correspondence. Eighty years later, Francis Kortheuer described the mutual dreams that formed the basis for their close and tender friendship:

> As little boys we had our fantasies which we kept secret from the adults, feeling that they would not approve of such dreamy nonsense. In our imagination we pictured ourselves as kings or rulers of our realms. Leo was king of his country—called it Colonora —and he drew maps of his country, plans of a city showing and naming the streets with train, car lines, etc. He also drew pictures of his ships and steamboats and men-of-war to fight the pirates! I did the same thing and called my country Columbia.

Railroads and boats were not only drawn and colored but also carved. Leo sailed his beautiful model yacht *Sylvia* on a small pond in Central Park; Frank fitted out the hull with a motor and battery to have it electrically propelled. Kortheuer continues in the same letter:

> He whittled our little model locomotives and cars and painted them to show the wheels, windows and names of railroads. These are quite small, about 3 inches long. I still have a few of them.

In later years Feininger not only built model ships as decorations for his room, but also, as mentioned previously, sailed them with his sons on the Baltic Sea. Many of the sailboats he drew and painted betray their origin in these models. He carved model trains and other objects for the children of his friends and once thought of working for the German toy industry. With the help of his wife and a friend he built a miniature theater for his family, with settings, figurines and electric lighting.[24] Charlotte Teller saw such a theater in his home in Berlin as well as "things that he had done when he was a lad of fifteen. They were minutely accurate and gave signs already of a mastery of draftsmanship."[25]

Indeed, we are told that at the age of five he drew from memory dozens of trains with all their details. Feininger's earliest known watercolor, a drawing of a locomotive, appears in his first letter to Kortheuer at his New York address, 430 West Fifty-seventh Street, on August 20, 1884, when Feininger was thirteen. It shows "Locomotive 37" with red wheels and is labelled: "This is a lightning express engine."[26] The same basic locomotive appears in much later paintings and woodcuts by Feininger. Thus, though Lyonel Feininger was trained for a career as a violinist when he came to Hamburg, he had already taken the first steps toward his true profession.

III
CARTOONING AND ILLUSTRATING

Student Years in Hamburg, Berlin, Liège, Paris

1887–1906

I left New York on the 13th of October on the Hamburgh American Company's steamer "Gellert." It was an old slowpoke doing remarkably well when it made 15 miles an hour. I was seasick all the way across. . . . On the 25th I reached Hamburgh and I am staying with a dear old maid [Miss J. Prealle] who is a devoted friend of Papa and Mama and who makes me call her Auntie. She is German but speaks *very* good English and so we understand each other perfectly. . . . We went to Berlin to see my father and mother, who were too busy to come to Hamburgh and who intended to see me at Christmas, after the concert tour was over. . . . Well I staid [sic] in Berlin two days. It is a beautiful city indeed, even the poorest streets are so beautifully clean and the horse cars stop only at certain stations. . . .

—Feininger to Kortheuer, November 4, 1887

Feininger wrote these words in his first letter from 66 Mühlendamm, Hamburg, at a critical point in his life. "Dumped there as a kid"[1] by his parents, as he put it in another letter, he was to enter art school less than a month after his arrival.

When his biographers refer to his choice of art as a profession they use the phrase "He drifted into art," probably quoting Feininger himself, who never really accounted for the step. The fullest description of the circumstances surrounding his entry into art school is given by Wight.[2] Feininger told him that originally it had been his goal to study at the Leipzig Conservatory, his father's old school. "His intended teacher was out of the country. Waiting in Hamburg young Feininger drifted into art school and never went to Leipzig."

It seems that the arts and crafts school was a compromise. Lyonel, then sixteen, had not completed his formal education. He

23

had attended grammar school number sixty-nine on Fifty-fourth Street in New York for two years, then left it to work in Wall Street as a messenger boy and to study violin with his father. The art school gave him the opportunity to perfect his German while he was occupied in a way that suited his talents—the neatly executed drawings and watercolors which he had brought with him from America clearly show his artistic aptitude. Earlier, he and Kortheuer had both received some special art training from "Aunt" Hilda Marshall, who had been a pupil of William Chase at the Art Students League, New York. This instruction was chiefly in charcoal drawing from still lifes.

The Hamburg School, chiefly designed to promote minute skill and to train craftsmen, was neither better nor worse than other institutions of the kind at this time. Feininger does not name his teachers there, but we gain some information from the autobiography of the sculptor Ernst Barlach,[3] who attended the school at about the same time in 1888. He tells us that his first drawing teacher, Herr Woldemar, the Dane, a pupil of Barthel Thorvaldsen, was a "regular Super-Teuton, a power-drunk berserk," and he calls the time spent at the school "the year of Calamity 1888." For Feininger and his parents, however, studying art at a regular school of some sort must have seemed an attractive temporary expedient.

In that first letter to Kortheuer, young Feininger used cartoons and drawings as well as words to introduce his friend to his new surroundings. The drawings are of a German express train and a local double-decker street-car; one of the cartoons shows "the dear old maid's" vicious talking parrot and the other, "Feininger in the bathtub with lighted ship-candle."

In the second letter, written the following February in 1888, he told of his entry into art school in November 1887, and decorated the envelope with "Feininger's new artist's flag," emblazoned with palette and brush. Life had now become serious.

I am not being permitted to write to anyone but my parents and sisters, once a week, on account of working eight hours a day in drawing school. . . . I am going to be an artist (painter). . . .

I do not see an English word except my handwriting (see how miserably I spell) and it is getting hard for me to speak english except simplified like a german who speaks pretty correct, but accented english.

So he asked Kortheuer to send him a sea tale. The two friends had read *Around the World in Eighty Days* together, and some novels by Dickens, James Fenimore Cooper, and Bret Harte. Feininger particularly enjoyed Cooper's *The Pilot* and *The Rover*. His interest in sea and adventure stories continued throughout his formative years in Europe. In a letter to Kortheuer, April 2, 1894, Feininger stated that his small personal library contained: "Four of Cooper's Sea Tales, 3–4 Dickens, Bret Harte (one of my favorites). Have read Conan Doyle's 'Sherlock Holmes,' admire Stevenson's vivid fantasy greatly." By this time, according to his letters, he had further read *Gulliver's Travels, Robinson Crusoe, Don Quixote* and Mark Twain's *Life on the Mississippi*. In the late nineties he developed a love of Russian and Polish writers, and became particularly intrigued by George Du Maurier's *Trilby*, which reminded him of situations he had come across during his first stay in Paris. In a letter to Kortheuer of May 19, 1898, Feininger expressed his liking for Rudyard Kipling's tales.

Feininger continued to mention his old technological interests —drawing and carving trains and boats, drafting maps of imaginary kingdoms, news of "elevated railroad smashups, fires, yacht races, and challenges for the America's Cup."[4] Sailing still fascinated him.

Aware that Frank loved it too, he described this scene for him in a letter of April 4, 1888:

I wish to write you a description of the two lakes in Hamburg! You can refer to the enclosed map. There are fine houses on every side of the big or outer Alster as it is called, and business houses on the inner Alster. Steamboats like the enclosed picture run constantly from and to different little docks, making about 6 to 8 miles an hour but very pleasant (school time!) The water is almost chock full of rowboats, and little sailing yachts, among which are a few American ones, so exquisitely beautiful in model and rig that they are always to be known from the german's! The English and Americans build the best, fastest and handsomest ships in the world and for speed America has no peer. These fine American boats are always winning over the germans and of course they get sort of mad but it is good to show them that there is someone better than they, for they are awfully stuck up.

And he hastened to add:

Well! I do miss the boat lake in Central Park. I sold my beautiful racer "Sylvia" for one dollar! . . . Do you ever go to the boat lake. If so, I expect you may see her there. . . How is captain? If you see him *do please* tell him I think of him and send him my love. He will know Leo. So will almost anyone else, the old watchman included, for, upward of two years no one was seen oftener there than I.

The art school began to absorb Feininger more and more, and he proudly informed Kortheuer:

There is to be an exhibition at Easter at my school and only the works of the best scholars will be represented and I am trying very hard to make my things perfect and my teacher also asked me help him hang and arrange the paintings, drawings et cetera of his class. Of course I am perfectly delighted and it is certainly very unusual that he asked me as I have been with him only *since November* and the others several years but he takes a great interest in me, I can see, and talks with me almost like a friend while the others never talk with him. . . . I speak German now almost perfectly and can understand everything that is said, but *cannot* write or spell at all, though I read quite well. Will you be a painter and my comrade through life? . . . I love it and am so determined as to my future calling that life would seem not worth struggling through it, if I could not follow this calling . . . Oh! Oh! a beard and a slouch hat and live in a *warm* climate where one can take pleasure in the open air instead of having to always wear rubbers, overcoat and carry a parasol as here in Hamburgh and wear ear muffs.

It is interesting to observe how the child and the adolescent in Feininger struggled with each other during these months in

Hamburg. Similarly, memories of America contended with the influences of his new German surroundings. This struggle was evident in the deterioration of his English and expressed itself in his cartoon style, which began more and more to resemble that of the German caricaturist, Wilhelm Busch. Only the meticulously clean and expert manner in which he drew trains and boats remained the same as before.

I have really something to be thankful for inasmuch that *no* one tells *me*, I am ten years too old to play with my stone blocks, a Christmas present from Auntie Prealle.

After this assertion of his right to linger in childhood, he immediately continued with a report of his success in the crafts school student exhibit.

I helped my teacher at the exhibition. . . . I have been promoted to upper class by the *director* himself . . . he told his clerk that I had made "riesige fortschritt." . . . In the middle class I used to copy and paint landscapes in aquarell (I will be an *aquarell* painter or none!) and let the people try it themselves who think it easy, to paint an accurate copy, with clear correct coloring. I drew hands from plaster, shading them with technical shading (Ask Aunt Hilda what that means) and ornaments from plaster, which I shaded with black shades of india ink, I mean from almost white to black, *not* in solid black. In the upper class I will paint from still life (aquarell) draw heads of beautiful Greek Gods and Hm, Hm *Goddesses* (that will be a pleasure for I love to draw them) and compose ornaments and titles, borders and all sorts of artistic designs. I will tell you how many I had in the exhibition. I had thirteen, XIII, 13, and that was more than any other boy had in the exhibition and our school has over 3000 scholars (though some come in the night school, some only on Sundays).

How prophetic was his resolution to become a water color landscapist "or none"; how naïve his anticipation of drawing "heads of beautiful Greek Gods and Hm, Hm *Goddesses*."

The same letter contained drawings of trains, a "complete list of the Ocean Navigation Companies in Colonora," and a clipping of a wood engraving titled "Locomotive Atlantic" 1832, "aus Thurston Die Dampfmaschine" (from Thurston's *The Steam Engine*).

In the middle of the year 1888 Feininger moved to Berlin. Since his parents had left this town where Lyonel had briefly visited them from Hamburg, he boarded with a German family. Meanwhile his parents went on a long concert tour—their last— to Brazil.

But young Feininger loved his independence and was glad about the change in his circumstances. He wrote about it to Kortheuer:

I am now in Berlin away from Auntie (Thank God!) and am studying in a studio in order to pass examination in the academy in October. I draw only masks and after living models and get along surprisingly.

The cartoons enclosed in this first letter from Berlin dated July 28, 1888, are very dependent on the style of Wilhelm Busch, though his name is not yet mentioned. Feininger entitled the cartoons *The new Hose, Punishment of Greedyguttiness, Retribution: A Romance,* and said in the text, "I enclose the caricatures only to show that I have improved immensely."

This short letter was followed by a longer one written the next day:

I am entirely at liberty out of my study hours, to draw, read, write letters, play violin; whatever I like. . . . I caricature almost all my spare time and have many fine caricature books from which I learn very much. I have improved greatly haven't I? You look back at my earlier caricatures and you will see that it was sheer luck if any of the figures had fun or expression in them. Only since my birthday when I got these books, have I commenced to improve, but have studied the style and all, *not* copying of course, but learning and so in this last week alone have I made great improvement. It is a favorite amusement of mine now.

This letter also contained cartoons in the rounded, abbreviated style of Busch, detailed pen drawings of boat races, and a watercolor of an express locomotive.

Between August 13 and September 27, 1888, Lyonel wrote and illustrated a series of eleven postcards (addressed from Lützow Platz 6, Berlin W. 62, care of Herr Regierungsrat Meitzner). The lines run vertically as well as horizontally, sometimes overlapping each other, sometimes in red, sometimes in black ink. Five of the cards were illustrated with trains and boats, the rest with caricatures. The caricatures included the previously mentioned *Violinist*, drawn much larger than most of Feininger's other cartoon figures. A minutely drawn king retiring for the night bears the caption, "Even the Bed (Ahem) insects welcome the Majesty." The third, a proposed addition to the *Pranks of Max and Moritz* introduces them: "These two are called Max and Moritz." The fourth, similar to Busch's pretentious and inept paint-splasher, "Maler Klexel," is a cartoon of an artist with a slouch hat and a huge portfolio. As a budding painter himself, Feininger was especially fond of poking fun at such types. The same character re-appears as a watercolor in the Churchill scrapbook. The remaining two postcards are also carried out in the manner of Busch.

This outburst of Buschian humor came quite late in Feininger's development as a cartoonist. It is rather strange that he seems not to have known Busch's *Max and Moritz* before he came to Berlin, since this children's classic, first published in 1865 in Munich, had been translated into many languages (first English translation Boston, 1871, by Charles T. Brooks); it gained great popularity in the United States and must have been widely read in German-American nurseries.

Wilhelm Busch was first mentioned by Feininger in a letter to Kortheuer on March 8, 1890:

I am going to send you one of Wilhelm Busch's german karikatur books. They are not very finely drawn but they are very full of life and humor. The American caricatures are the best in the world. You will see lots of them in *Judge* drawn by "Zim." He is really wonderful and if you buy *Judge* look out for his drawings.

A year after he started to work in the style of Busch, Feininger, although increasingly critical of "Zim" (Eugene Zimmerman), returned to the American manner of cartoon drawing, which at that time still followed the considerable example of George Cruikshank, the British caricaturist and Dickens illustrator. Both cartoon styles depended on comic exaggeration, but Busch's lines were bold, simple, and rounded, while Cruikshank's were exacting, detailed, almost illustrative.

Lyonel wavered artistically and emotionally between Germany and America. While he praised his "freedom" in the Berlin boarding house, he lamented:

How tired I am of germany! Oh how homesick I am after New York and Dear old America! Dear me: Wait until you go in a strange country and feel ready to burst with longing after old friends and places and you will feel just as I do.[5]

He recalled vacations at Lake George in New York, autumn in America, sailboat races, and "jolly Indian fights" with neighborhood boys.[6] Enclosed with the letter were two marvelous watercolor maps of his dream countries, "Marina" and "Alvrancibra," as well as a meticulously executed watercolor of *The Alvrancibra Elevated*, showing a train passing over a bridge, one of the chief symbols of Feininger's art. However, this nostalgia and fantasy did not interfere with his preparations for the entrance examinations at the Academy and his attempts to earn money by contributing illustrations and caricatures to newspapers.

In a postcard to Kortheuer on June 29, 1889, Lyonel announced his success in both endeavors. The card was decorated with a caricature representing himself as extremely thin and spindly-necked, wearing a slouch hat and black goggles—the last a recent acquisition to aid eyes weakened by his tiny writing and drawing.

I work very much for the caricature papers here and have also a great many orders for drawings of different subjects. I made a brilliant examination at the Academy and was accepted after the first week, while all the rest of the candidates had to work 5 weeks and then out of 90 only 9 came in. Next year I hope to get to Muenchen or Munich, and study landscape painting.

You can anyway see that I am "booming." I am going to send some drawings in to "Judge" in New York.

Some of Feininger's earliest cartoons which were published by Berlin newspapers in 1889 (with German captions) have been preserved by Mr. Kortheuer. Two of them are concerned with the humor of children. One is called *A Materialistic Bud,* the other *Progress.* The translation of the caption for the second cartoon reads:

Lawyer: Hey, little one, what is the matter?
Elsa (four years old): Boo-hoo (crying) I insist on a divorce
    from my parents, boo-hoo!

The idea might have come from his own unhappy family life. The style in both is more American than German, reminding one some-what of "Zim." Despite his success with the German newspapers, it is significant to note that he also planned to send some drawings to the American magazine, *Judge,* although the only caricature with an English caption (in the Churchill scrapbook) intended for *Judge* is of two starved Irish characters "who have not eaten for so long, they could hardly find their mouth."

The cartoon which most closely presaged Feininger's later caricatures in text and style is captioned "The Editor of the Future. He writes, edits, illustrates, and prints his own paper." The calendar shows the date 1939, fifty years ahead. The room is crowded with weird but possible mechanical contraptions. The editor has a hooked nose, wears striped pants à la Uncle Sam and is surrounded by a box of Havana cigars, beer on tap, a telephone, and a device which foreshadows the dictaphone. On the left is Feininger's early monogram. Though period-bound, the style of this cartoon, which Feininger designated as "one of my first drawings," seems to be even more American than the others.

A new chapter in Feininger's life began when he entered the Royal Prussian Art Academy in Berlin during the winter of 1888. He continued his correspondence with Kortheuer, but these letters now merely supplement his observations and confidences to

Alfred Vance Churchill, whom Feininger had met shortly after he entered the Academy. The first item pasted on the inside cover of Churchill's scrapbook of items relating to their friendship is a slightly retouched reproduction of an ink drawing in Feininger's Buschian style signed and dated *Léonell Feininger fecit 14.XI.88.* It contains humorous symbols and scenes of the life of artists and shows St. Lucas, the patron saint of painters, perched on top of an old German building (fig. 4).

On May 20, 1890, Feininger wrote his first letter to Churchill, who was then staying in Paris. This letter (addressed from "Unter den Linden 16"), as well as others from the year 1890, was decocated with caricatures—Feininger's chief interest and a modest source of livelihood. The examples of his earliest cartoon style in these letters have relatively few supernatural elements despite his early inclination toward the fantastic. Instead they tend to follow in mood (though not always in style and subject) the cozy Biedermeier tradition represented at that time by the *Fliegende Blätter* (*The Flying Sheets*), the oldest and most famous of the early German satirical magazines (published in Munich since 1848). The influence of the greatest genius among the German caricaturists, Wilhelm Busch, was still occasionally apparent, as in a *Self Portrait of Feininger at the School Desk Learning the French Alphabet* (dated Liège, October 7, 1890).

The pen and ink drawings in these letters from Liège were part German and part American in style although their subject matter usually had an American flavor. In a letter from Liège on November 16, Feininger represented his "bucolic friend Churchill on his native heath" smoking a corncob pipe, with tall stalks of corn in the background. Two drawings in this letter from Liège which seem even more characteristic of Feininger's graphic humor foreshadowed his later work in their mixture of music with fantastic mechanisms. One of them is not only the wittiest and most inventive but the most elaborately executed of these early cartoons. The caption reads *Al Practising Upon the Typewriter in a Fit of Abstraction plays a Bach Praeludium and Fuga.* The second

4. Cover illustration for *Fest-Zeitung.* 1888.

shows the effects of his "cramming" for school: it is captioned *Leo's Cubiform Head, in the New York Museum of Un-Natural History.*

Earlier, Feininger had proudly announced to his new friend that he had repeatedly received orders for five or six drawings at a time from the Berlin weekly founded in 1884, *Humoristische Blätter* (*Humorous Sheets*), and that he had illustrated "a story, an episode of a wintry night, supposed to take place in a cellar." For these drawings and similar work he had earned 217 marks, a tidy sum at that time. Yet he was aware that even the highly finished drawings in his "best style" were only "potboilers":

I make very few fantasies. That will come again though, for I am getting to be a regular storehouse of the most vivid, horrible drastic chiaro oscuro effects man ever saw or dreamed of—of course unpeopled, for my imagination generally fails to conjure up figures drastic enough for their surroundings.

Even at this early point in his career he had hoped that he could find a market for his particular kind of humor, satire, and fantasy in the United States. In a letter of June 11, 1890, he wrote:

When I go to America I shall go to work for *Life* and a few other journals and try to earn a competence for myself. As an auxiliary I may possibly enter the broker's office in Wall Street of a dear friend of my father's where I already have been for a year, and between the hours of 9 A.M. and 3:30–4 P.M. daily earn 7 or 8 dollars a week, and draw in the evenings and on Sunday.

The old *Life* (founded in 1883 by J. A. Mitchell and E. S. Martin) attacked the foibles of high society and, as William A. Murrell puts it in his *History of American Graphic Humor*, "played the role of *arbiter elegantiarum*."[7] Earlier New York humor magazines like *Puck* (founded in 1877) and *Judge* (founded in 1881) had a more definitely political character. *Puck's* first editor, the versatile Viennese emigrant Joseph Keppler, had earlier started a German-language magazine in St. Louis. In New York, in partnership with Adolph Schwartzman, he was almost immediately successful with both the German and the English editions of his paper.

It is interesting to note that many of the artists employed by these humor magazines were German or Austrian by birth or descent. Their illustrations—chiefly lithographs and wood engravings —show some of the ideas and stylistic mannerisms of the old country, where cartooning had been an offspring of the political revolution. Young Feininger, himself a descendant of "old '48" revolutionaries, must have been attracted by the political humor in these weeklies. Two things promised him a successful career as a magazine and newspaper artist: his familiarity with the field of cartooning, and the fact that the leading American newspapers had employed cartoonists regularly since the mid-1890's, when colored Sunday comic supplements had been made possible by the invention of the multicolor printing press.

The first legitimate newspaper cartoon series was drawn by R. F. Outcault. It appeared for the first time on Sunday, November 18, 1894, in the Sunday Supplement of Joseph Pulitzer's *New York World* with the caption "Origin of a New Species, or the Evolution of the Crocodile explained." About one year later, Outcault began another series for the same paper called "Down in Hogan's Alley" which featured America's first popularly sucessful cartoon character, "The Yellow Kid." The cartoon seemed to have a great future in America, and Feininger felt that he was the man to give it a specific style.

The Kortheuer letters of 1890 tell of these plans and hopes and of his resolution to return to New York at the earliest opportunity. In a letter of March 8, 1890, written from Berlin, Feininger wrote that he was "now a regular carikaturist for the Berlin papers," but not happy despite his success: "I am very homesick after America and I like Germany always less and less. In fact I consider it as a prison and would give anything to get back to America."

This remark was followed by a cartoon showing Germany as a kind of Alcatraz surrounded by water separating it from America, which appears in the distance as a beautiful mountain

5. A *"Germanized Irishman."* Pen cartoon. 1893.

range (fig. 6). The letter is decorated at the bottom of the last page with a drawing of a painter—a halo hovering above his head —working at his easel. It is signed *Your loving Friend Leo, Emperor of Colonora.*

The next letter to Kortheuer, written on April 16, also spoke of his hard work for the Berlin papers:

Soon I will be able to earn my living! I am almost 19 years old now and have grown so that I am sure you never would know me. . . . I am about 5 feet 9 or 10 inches high. . . . Today some more of my drawings were printed, 4 sketches, showing an acrobat on a 4th class car and how he falls over as the train starts suddenly. . . .

I learned pen drawing all alone . . . and I am prouder of that fact, and take more pleasure in pen drawing than anything else. . . .

I have made lots of drawings from jokes or subjects of my own, but now I am saved the trouble for it *is* a nuisance, having to think out one's own jokes, for the people now send me the ideas, short stories, jokes and poems to illustrate.

Four sketches enclosed with this letter—*The Groundfloor Acrobat on a Journey*—are preserved in Kortheuer's scrapbook. The subject is characteristic of Feininger's bizarre humor during his adolescent phase. The style and subject matter fuse elements of American and German caricature, as in his sketch of a Germanized Irishman, very tall with thin legs and enormous shoes (fig. 5), possibly a partial, mocking self-portrait, whose likeness appears again in the *Assembly of the Bearded Sons of Germania* (*Vereinigung der bärtigen Söhne Germanias,* fig. 7).

Later, Feininger vigorously repudiated this work done under pressure and mostly from other people's ideas; but when he began to work for the papers he enjoyed being busy, close to contemporary life, and affecting it with the creations of his pen. In a cartoon in a letter of April 6, he showed in drawing and text "How busy I will be in about a year from now, so that I will be compelled to hire a truck to take my sketches to the papers as soon as I make them."

The proclivity for pictorial journalism was a common trait

...ped it so much, I cant begin to tell you how much pleasure it has ... me. Would you (could you) send me "The water witch" or "Red ...? I miss them so much and should dearly love to have them, ... would! Would you be so kind? Do you wear long pants yet? Last night I was at a ball and did not get home until 4 oclock this morning. I do not feel extra well and just before I commenced this letter I disgorged myself as you see in the sketch below. I feel a little better since but still am not quite up to the mark. Dearest Frankie I am going to send you one of Wilhelm Busches german caricatur books. They are not very finely drawn but they are very full of life and humor. The american caricatures are the ... in the world. You will see lots of them in Judge, drawn by ...". He is really wonderful and if you buy a Judge look out for his drawings. Do you still collect Stamps? I have so little time to attend to my collection that I hardly have looked at my book these 2 years. I have about 3000 stamps though, and severall exceedingly rare ones, notably from Persia and the British colonies, also Portug... ...ese colonies. I am very homesick after America and I like

Germany always less and less. In fact I begin to consider it as a prison and would give anything to get back to America. How is Arthur? He must ... very big now. Plea... give him my love ... Also your father a... Aunt Flora and Grandma Knott.

Dear Frankie you must excuse me that write so stupidly and uninterestingly, but I am very distracted with bad headache. I skated a great deal this winter and can skate very well now. Do you also skate? Down below you see me skating. I suppose you know that I am shortsighted and wear specs. I look like a proffessor, as you can see by the enclosed Photograph which I had taken at New years! each ... I suppose you gave up all hope of ever other getting one from me. What do you haven to think I look like now! I have changed ...? I very much since we last saw ... tell yo... a great secret! I have a little ... mustasch no... and when we see each other again you will hardly know me.

6. Letter to H. Francis Kortheuer. 1890.

7. *Association of the Bearded Sons of Germany*
(*Vereinigung der bärtigen Söhne Germanias*). Pen cartoon. 1893.

among American artists like Feininger who were starting their careers in the last decade of the nineteenth century. Not only did such work provide some financial return for the beginner, but it also satisfied the American interest in the events and the rapidly accelerating pace of the time. The "Eight of 1908"–the famous "Ashcan School" of American realists–was comprised of a group of former newspaper artists. Like the members of the Ashcan group, Feininger also moved from newspaper drawing to free oil painting. However, even if he had returned to America in the nineties, it is doubtful that his art would have developed in a style similar to that of the "Eight"; his bias toward fantasy would soon have directed him away from mere scene painting.

When his father promised to let him return to New York in June of 1890, Feininger simultaneously reported the good news to his two friends. He used almost the same words to both and decorated the communications with the same caricature. It shows *Feininger on the Tramp,* a foot-sore hobo under a sign that reads *For America.* The postcard to Kortheuer stated:

I have a piece of grand news for you, that is, there is every chance for its happening: That is, I am coming to America in September!!!! I hope my father won't change his mind. He is in New York all alone. I suppose you know, and told me I might come to live with him. His address is 164 East 81st.

The next day he wrote to Churchill, who had previously informed Feininger of his own planned return to America:

So I am too. I go in September unless my father goes back on his promise which I received a week ago. . . . When I go to America I will have not money enough to stop in London. We are all hard up and poor people at present. . . . I can imagine you in rapturous silence before a Turner, say for instance 'whalers caught in the ice, boiling blubber.' . . .

Feininger envied his friends their art junkets through the galleries of Europe. On a postcard sent to Paris (the Churchills' next stop), he made a whimsical pen drawing of the couple dressed in exaggerated tourist costume. The caption on the drawing reads: *The young Churchill couple as tourists in Paris.*

But the visit of Karl Feininger to his family in Berlin in the summer of 1890 had an unexpected outcome for young Feininger which destroyed his plans to work for *Life* in New York. His father sent Lyonel away to the Jesuit college of St. Gervais in Liège, Belgium.[8] The reason for this decision was that Lyonel had pawned his watch to help a friend. Feininger recalled this "catastrophe" and the way his aroused father treated him as "the lost sheep" of the family in a letter he wrote more than fifty years later to his musician friend Fred Werner.[9] Lyonel and Werner had belonged to the same circle of young Berlin artists whom Karl Feininger suspected of bohemian tendencies. It is probable that the "innocent crime" of pawning the watch was merely a pretext for Karl to remove his son from these influences and at the same time to further his neglected formal education. The father now insisted that Lyonel finish school. Since neither parent had ever attempted to give him a religious education, a Catholic college seemed a good choice. Feininger's younger sisters had spent two years in a Belgian convent school.

Feininger arrived in Liège on September 2 and remained there for less than a year. His cartoons—some of which have been discussed earlier—show that his initial resentment of the school led to situations somewhat beneath the dignity of a nineteen-year-old budding artist.[10] Nevertheless, as he told Churchill in a letter of January 27, 1891, the school gave him

a new revelation of the duties of my life . . . making a very new old Feininger under the guidance of the excellent Reverend Fathers. . . . But being here for my future good, it is advisable to not merely learn French . . . but lay some sort of a foundation of a moral sort. My father wishes it, and I am beginning myself to see into it.

Feininger, who regarded himself as "fundamentally religious," here acknowledged his indebtedness to the guidance of the Jesuits, whom he occasionally portrayed in later pictures.[11]

The impressions of medieval architecture which he gathered in Belgium proved of still greater consequence in the development of Feininger's later art. For Feininger, as for Henry Adams, Belgian Gothic was his first encounter with the aesthetic aspect of old Europe. Both men felt a delighted surprise at the contrast in this architecture to that of their native America. The medieval fairyland of towns, turrets, walls, moats, bridges, stepped gables, and slender steeples which had impressed him so much as a child on the gold-leaf panels of the Metropolitan Museum was here, all wondrously preserved. Love of the medieval never again left him; it led to his superb "architectural fugues" of Halle and Lüneburg in the twenties.

During that summer Feininger visited Brussels and studied its monuments every evening under the expert guidance of a Professor Kloth with whom he stayed. A drawing of *Léo in Brussels*, depicting Feininger standing at night before a Gothic church portal (fig. 8), accompanied a letter to Churchill (Oct. 7, 1890) in which he described his impressions:

I was a week in that most beautiful Old city: Brussels. . . . The streets are narrow, for the most part hilly, even mountainous at places and winding. . . . At night is the time to see this Paris in miniature, as it is called, for then the streets are like the halls of a gigantic castle, lighted up for a grand reception, and the by-streets seem like lesser apartments in which to retreat and cool and refresh oneself before again going into the glaring thoroughfares. The streets are used as well as the sidewalks and there are but few wagons. . . . There the quaint old houses, three and four centuries old, some of them with their huge chimneys and quaint gables, give existence in their darker recesses to monstrous shadows from the dazzling lights, which make them, the houses, appear quite unlike other houses. Of course the wonderful old Rathaus [the city hall] and beautiful weather-stained, weather-beaten cathedral are the chief buildings and I couldn't grow weary of gazing at them.

It is characteristic that this sensitive description of old houses, huge chimneys, quaint gables, and monstrous shadows took precedence over the more spectacular sights of the city hall and the

...that most beautiful old city; Brussels!! What a
wonderful old place it is! Oh Al! if you could only
[be] with me now, and see Brussels! The streets are narrow
[for] the most part, hilly, even mountainous at places, and
winding. The stores are princely, as to the goods displayed,
[an]d the generally old buildings they adorn are rendered
[entirely] subservient to the display of their riches. At night
[is] the time to see this Paris in
miniature, as it is called, for then
[the] streets are like the halls of a
gigantic Castle, lighted up for a grand
[rec]eption, and the bye streets, seem
[li]ke lesser apartments in which to
[re]treat and cool and refresh one
[se]lf before again going into the glaring thoroughfares. The
[st]reets are used, as well as the sidewalks, and there are but
[fe]w wagons. Then the quaint old houses, three and four
[ce]nturys old, some of them, with their huge chimneys
[an]d quaint gables, give existence in their darker recesses
[to] monstrous shadows from the dazzling lights, which
[m]ake them, the houses, appear quite unlike other houses.
[Of] course the wonderful old Rathhaus and beautiful,
[we]ather stained, weather beaten cathedral are the
[ch]ief buildings, and I couldn't grow weary of gazing
[at] them. I have a very kind friend in Brussels, in
[th]e person of Professor Rloth, with whom I remained
[w]hile there; who showed me around the town every
[e]vening, and rendered my stay there like a fairy dream

see in Brussels in the night-time.

whenever I recall it. I cannot think of the days; but
the remembrance of those nights! There! I have finish[ed]
my ecstasy over this wonderful old city, although I could go on for[ever]
but why?: the pen is cold; and gives no idea. We have play ti[me]
between each lesson, and what do you think we play with?
as you would never guess it, I
ha-ha-ha! ha-ha-he-ho-hoho,
you! we play, man and child, e[ach]
one of us with hoops! At first [it]
seemed too, too, too utterly indik[e]
but now I am used to it I can sa[y]
that I should anywhere, warmly
defend its use as a healthy, frien[dly]
sport. We play Tag, each trying to run down the others [?]
with his own, and this permits of considerable adroitness
Above, I have been trying to express the first impress[ion]
of one, of seeing a man 20 years old chasing a hoop
with a stick. There are many amusing accidents, and n[o]
one is ever angry about it, either: for instance: a boy is
hard pressed, while playing tag, by the fellow who is "it"
All at once, the chaser will slide his hoop after the f[irst]
one, and the hoop mixes itself
up with his legs and throws him,
or, if he has luck, he staggers up
to a wall and untangles himself
from the hoop as best he can.
see this attempt at a sketch
to illustrate the ludicrousness of the aforesaid acci[dent]
but it aint much of a success I fear. I was in a great...

8. Letter to Alfred Vance Churchill. 1890.

cathedral. Perhaps even more important, this first vivid impression of a medieval city was received at night: "I cannot think of the days, but those nights," Feininger wrote in the same letter.

In words and drawings, Feininger described similar medieval subjects in Liège:

> I have a great choice of subject here, both in ancient streets and wondrous old walls, buildings, etc. and human caricatures or rather character studies in the working class and the peasants . . . old Dutch barges from Ostende and Antwerpen.[12]

In a letter of November 24 he described the color effects of the quaint old houses with a peculiar sensitivity which anticipated the feeling in his later work, especially in the water colors:

> The inhabitants here have the adorable custom of first painting their houses with chalky colors and leaving them to mellow down in delicious tints by wind and rain, none of your elegant grey streets as in our dear but sadly modern Berlin. Oh Al what straw roofs I have seen a short way out of town, during our class promenades! Now tell me, do you see such things in America as straw roofs? Ain't the country too criminally rich to offer such luxuries to the artist's eye and too modern to show buildings of the 11th and 12th centuries?

Feininger's remarks about "tone" and about the reasons for the distortion of a high, exaggerately slender old house—"to fit the picture"—are recorded on the back of a pencil sketch, dated September 19, 1890, in the Detroit Archives scrapbook. A second drawing of the same subject, this time in ink, identifies this quaint high house, which looks like a medieval watchtower, as a "Café" (fig. 9). This tower must have impressed him, because there is still a third version of it preserved in the Churchill scrapbook. Feininger used light green tone paper this time, rather than his usual light brown. As was his custom at that time, he heightened the drawing with Chinese opaque white. It is dated Liège, November 26, 1890. It is from such early endeavors that the high houses in Feininger's later paintings derived, glowing with a mysterious transparency.

9. Café and houses in Liège.
Pen, Chinese white, colored paper. 1890.

10. Courtyard, Berlin. Watercolor. 1889.

Europe's charms enticed him. The bewitched artist began to forget his native land. Preoccupation with cartoons stopped for a time; he ended a letter to Churchill: "Let us talk rather of landscape, in which we both have our principal sympathies as well as our aspirations, rather than caricature. I am very content and even happy here."

In his landscape sketches Feininger strove most eagerly for atmosphere and mood. Though most of his work at that time was still in black and white, he tried to give it a colorful look by using tone paper and Chinese white. Characteristic passages dealing with technique appear in his letters to Churchill from Belgium.

Liège, October 7, 1890:

Have you ever tried sketching on *tone* paper? and getting the lighter portions with Chinese white? You would be astonished how simple and effective a method it is. I tried it only lately, here in Liège, when I had a couple of weeks vacation before the College opened, and it has completely changed my ideas on sketching in pencil. . . .

What useful, invaluable people these Chinamen are to us artists! What should we do without them? Chinese ink, Chinese white! . . .

I enclose a little sketch, on tone paper: by the way, I use 3 shades—lighter, medium, and dark—in keeping with the "Stimmung" [mood].

P.S. I never rub out lead pencil marks from the sketches! they are softer so!

November 16, 1890:

Much practice at careful penwork is a great thing. It helps one to recognize more easily the instinctive modelling of forms, giving them at once plasticity and motion, and the benefit does not rest alone with the pen, but extends its usefulness to brush and pencil. How I wish I could be out in Ohio with you, old man! I intend to, during the vacation, draw every day in and around Liège, not only on tone paper with pencil or brush, but I shall have my aquarell Kasten properly fitted up, and make watercolor studies for all I am worth.

Feininger now planned to take up graphic arts: "Etching is or should be the shrine of every religious painter who worships *Stimmung* and atmosphere" (letter from Liège, May 1, 1891). Churchill had previously directed Feininger's attention to the American etcher and watercolorist of cityscapes, Joseph Pennell,[13] who was then living in London. Thanking his friend for sending him reproductions of Pennell's work, Feininger wrote from Liège May 14, 1891:

> I am happy to have these Pennell sketches, they are fine, especially "Sundown in Oxford Street" and the "Towers of Westminster." I have heard you speak of Pennell, Abbey and other American illustrators, but, if you believe it, I had never before seen any work of Pennell.

Following his return to Berlin, Feininger again mentions Pennell in his letter to Churchill of June 15, 1891:

> Those Pennells and those wood engravings and the articles on Etching are invaluable to me for many reasons: raw as art ideas are in general in our own America; there exist true and noble men among our artists, and their ideas and teaching cannot but find echo in such a poor, humble aspirant as I feel myself more every day to be.

It is strange that Feininger failed to mention Whistler's name. But a statement he later made to Alfred H. Barr confirms the fact that Feininger knew his work at that time. Barr writes:

> Feininger knew Whistler's work during his early years in Germany and expressed his indebtedness in the following words: "I realized how much his paintings stood apart from those of his contemporaries in their simplification and purity of design. . . . These qualities, to a great degree, appealed to my own striving."[15]

The influence of Whistler can be seen in some drawings with Parisian motifs, such as *Green Sky and Yellow Houses;*[16] the title as well as the treatment recall Whistler's paintings and etchings of Venetian streets.

Feininger's admiration for Turner and Whistler, the two

masters of a vaporous, sketchy kind of painting, seems to clash with his preference for a clearly defining contour line which he was in the habit of practicing in his profession as a caricaturist and illustrator. These contrasting interests—love for the pictorial potentialities of color, and stress on line and its articulating, organizing function—ran parallel at that time with his often-confessed wavering between landscape and figure. A synthesis of color and line, landscape and figure was to be increasingly achieved in his later work after he had decided to become a free artist, but was not to be fully realized until the last years of his life, after his return to America.

During the formative years of his genius, Feininger reacted to all those outside influences which were in agreement with his own final aim as an artist—an aim at that time only dimly perceived. The graphic arts and painting in Europe and America, and the opportunity to study them in art publications, museums and exhibits, were then his chief interests. It was inevitable, then, that Feininger would be attracted to the movement that was bringing about a creative rejuvenation in virtually every field of the arts and crafts: *Art Nouveau*. Among other things, this movement established the freedom of the flowing line from the preceding historical styles, especially in the field of design, and it was no doubt this aspect of *Art Nouveau* that captured Feininger's interest at an early date. *Art Nouveau's* undular style spread quickly to the United States and during the early nineties found its centre in New York, in the manifold activities of Louis Comfort Tiffany.

This outstanding designer-craftsman introduced many revolutionary ideas and methods into the field of stained glass (in collaboration with the painter John La Farge), jewelry, and lamp design. In the spring of 1894, Feininger had viewed work by Tiffany at an exhibition of American crafts in Berlin. The German government had purchased some Tiffany pieces from the Columbian Exhibition at the Chicago World's Fair in the previous year. Tiffany had designed and built an entire chapel on the Fairgrounds, which was later installed in the cathedral of St. John the Divine in New

York City. With a certain pride in the achievements of his countryman, Feininger reported to Kortheuer from Berlin in 1894 on the "splendid glass windows and hanging electric lamp fixtures by the Tiffany Company, grating of copper and bronze for elevator doors of beautiful design and workmanship."

Toward the end of the century, *Art Nouveau,* as well as the art and aesthetics of Whistler, were rallying points for all anti-academic forces. Although Feininger was anxious to join in this battle between Design and Imitation, he was still too much engaged in the struggle for a living to yield fully to *Art Nouveau's* liberating forces. Eventually, of course, his new interest in etching in the manner of Pennell (the champion of Whistler in America) as well as his continued interest in the creative possibilities of watercolor landscapes combined to give Feininger a new vision of a promised land of artistic freedom.

Although Feininger's interest in etching and cityscape was lasting, after his return to Berlin at the end of May it became obscured by a renewed preoccupation with caricature, illustration, and the serious study of the human figure.

He had come to Berlin from Liège after his mother, who had established herself as a voice and piano teacher, had rented a flat for the family. In a letter to Churchill of June 15, 1891, Feininger described his new home with great affection. He saw this idyllic setting in the midst of a great city with the eyes of an artist trained to find compositional values and mood qualities in the design of overlapping roofs and differently lighted walls:

> We are living so beautifully now; we have a little flat of three rooms and kitchen, and I work by a window facing a charming little garden rich in trees and flowers, and with a surrounding of aristocratic-looking houses, not directly facing but standing off at quite a charming angle. I will sketch it one of these days and send it along to you.

This sketch, if he ever made it, is not extant; but he depicted a similar setting in an especially fine watercolor in the Churchill scrapbook (dated June 6, 1889). It radiates a mood of dreamy, aristocratic seclusion and peace (fig. 10).

48

Feininger favored architectural themes—windows, chimneys, geometrical patterns of overlapping forms, views of roofs from a high angle. His handling of the problems such subjects presented anticipated the masterful solutions of his later paintings. Architectural motifs appear in cartoons for the magazine *Ulk* (*Fun*), like *Policemen Training on the Roof*, Feb. 23, 1906.[17] A more serious two-color print, *Roofs in Snow*, was published in *Narrenschiff* (*Ship of Fools*) in 1898 (fig. 11).

In its poetic, melancholy, yet realistic treatment, it reflects the Berlin tradition of drawing then embodied in the art of Adolph von Menzel. It displays as well the flat, decorative tendencies of the graphic arts at the turn of the century.

Methods of art instruction as practised at the Royal Art Academy almost never took the beginning students out into the open. Instead, they were directed to draw from plaster casts; at best, they could do portraits. Instruction was freer and more progressive under a private tutor, who would usually consider everything in nature as a fitting subject for art work, stressing observation in outdoor study for his pupils. Feininger had looked in vain for this kind of training in the musty classroom of his first teacher at the Academy, Professor Ernst Hancke,[18] a dry realist of fifty-four who had little understanding of Feininger's talent.

Feininger had protested against the dulness and conventionality of the teaching in the official art academies. In a cartoon of 1889 (which he had sent to Kortheuer), a dwarf-like, impish art student stands before a typical art class object in such academies—a torso of a Greek goddess—and proudly displays his own creation to his aghast instructor: a bust of a grotesque creature with a nose like a baked potato. The instructor shrinks back from it in horror (fig. 12).

Feininger finally found the understanding he sought in the studio of Adolph Schlabitz.[19] He studied figure and life drawing under the independent tutor and accompanied him on sketching trips every Saturday.

During summer vacations he worked at home and sketched Berlin's picturesque riverfront (e.g., "Alt Berlin—Kölln am Wasser").

11. *Roofs in Snow* (*Dächer im Schnee*).
Two-color illustration for *Narrenschiff*. 1898.

He returned to these motifs in later years. Mrs. Julia Feininger's collection includes a very detailed study of a freighter resembling those that Feininger had observed on the Spree and the Berlin canals. It is done in soft pencil heightened with Chinese white, inscribed *Dead eye and lea board with fastenings,* and dated Sept. 6, 1892 (fig. 13).[20]

These flat, broad freighters anchored at the banks of the Havel and Spree rivers were favorite sketch subjects of Feininger and Churchill. They also did watercolors of them in friendly competition—a comparison of these pictures (in the Churchill scrapbook) clearly shows Feininger's superiority in the artistic and technical rendering of ships of all kinds. The drawings of waterfront houses in Old Berlin belong to the same category as those done by the two friends during their sketching trips.

Another carefully executed pencil drawing by Feininger dated two years later ("March 19, 1894, Am Kögel") shows a row of very old waterfront houses. In this drawing Feininger created a striking pattern with rows of windows shining in sunset light. He continued to be fascinated by this motif; eleven years later, on November 11, 1905, he wrote to his wife, "They act like mirrors and refract the rays of the setting sun like spears, thrown."

In the Berlin picture galleries he studied waterfront scenes in paintings by Eduard Hildebrandt (1818–1868) and Andreas Achenbach (1815–1910), both German followers of the Dutch and English landscape schools. In 1896 he mentioned the Karlsruhe landscapist Gustav Schoenleber (1815–1917) in a letter to Churchill, who had expressed a special interest in this artist. In the same letter, however, Feininger, then more inclined toward idealistic and fantastic figural compositions, called Makart and Böcklin "Kings in the realm of Fantasy." He had discovered the two in the Berlin museums after re-entering the Academy to study the human figure.

In the summer of 1891, while sketching on the Berlin streets, he tried his hand at figures in motion. He wrote Churchill on June 26:

12. Art student and instructor. Pen cartoon. 1889.

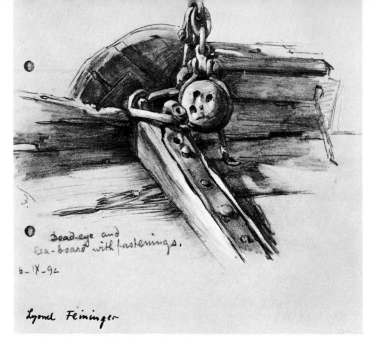

13. *Dead-eye and lea-board with fastenings.*
Pen and watercolor. 1892.

14. Illustration for
Brete Harte's "A Ship of '49."
Pen and watercolor. 1890.

Would it surprise you if I were to tell you, a propos of the little *Skizze ci-joint* [sketch attached], that I am doing quite a little work in this line: *Damenskizzen* [sketches of ladies], etc. . . . and find it a very interesting thing, needing much more grace and delicate drawing than anything I have hitherto attempted?

He concentrated on figure drawing during the following fall and winter. "There is nothing like the study from the nude for every quality that is paramount in drawing," he wrote on October 6 to Churchill, who had just assumed his first teaching position at Iowa (later Grinnell) College. In a congratulatory letter, Feininger wrote that his friend had undertaken "the noble mission . . . of pioneer at work in [his] own country." He informed Churchill that he too had achieved some success by re-entering the Berlin Academy and had been admitted to "the highest drawing class," the so-called *Antiken Klasse* under Professor Woldemar Friedrich,[21] "where only nudes from nature and after statues are drawn." He added: "Now Friedrich is *anerkannt* [acknowledged] the best teacher at the Academy. . . . Portrait-*zeichnen* [drawing] is over for me—old Hancke a vision of the past." Through Woldemar Friedrich, Feininger became a direct legatee of the Berlin tradition in drawing, since Friedrich was a pupil of Steffeck, who had studied with Franz Krüger, who in turn had influenced Menzel.

At that time (1891) Feininger's portrait was drawn in pencil by another American, F. Coburn, a fellow student at the Academy. "It is not too much of a likeness but it will pass for me," he wrote, "and besides you can see how Leo has grown 'Cutlets' [sideburns]. They make Leo quite respectable, so the girls say." The profile drawing is preserved in the Churchill scrapbook. When compared to photographs taken at that time, it seems a fairly good likeness. We know them likewise from the Detroit scrapbook. One of them bears the dedication *My beloved Alfred von seinem Herzensbruder* [from his heart's brother] *Leonell Feininger*. Feininger was soon, at least acording to his own estimate, "way the first" in the *Antiken Klasse* and "one of the best in the whole concern." Such classes were a traditional feature in German art academies. The advanced students drew nudes from life as well as plastercasts representing masterpieces of ancient statuary.

Despite his success in this field, Feininger began to doubt the direction his studies were taking. In a letter of January 12, 1892, he revealed to his "only Bruderseele [soul-brother] . . . met with in our art" that: "The longer I keep at figure drawing the more I feel a longing after landscape, and although I make good progress in the former, I feel I was not born to it."

His success with his teacher Friedrich, who "has no fear for the future" did not blind him to the shortcomings of academic teaching: "No composition and ideas over what *elements* are necessary in a picture, in order that it has *meaning* and *inwardness*" are taught, "not a single thought is paid." This becomes a statement of great significance when one considers the ever-growing tendency toward analytical and metaphysical treatment of subjects in Feininger's artistic development.

His drawing ability and the reputation he enjoyed at the Academy made it easy for him to get commissions and to earn money. He wrote to his friend that he had been commissioned:

> . . . to illustrate a novel, at 15 marks a drawing. The second large order is to make cigar box etiquettes, being for about 250 drawings . . . *"Romanillustrationen"* [story illustrations] which I am making for the "Berliner Illustrierte Zeitung." . . . I have to do violence to my imagination . . . for they are illustrations to a "Hintertreppen Roman" [backstairs novel].

Several preliminary sketches are in Churchill's scrapbook, as well as photographs of the published illustrations for these melodramatic thrillers. Feininger refers to them in a letter he wrote to Churchill on October 7, 1890, shortly after he had begun his stay in Liège.

His letter also deals with his more satisfying attempts to illustrate short stories and poetry of a vastly higher literary calibre: "Before leaving Berlin, which I did on the 8th September, I made several illustrations to a book of Bret Harte's 'A ship of 49' for old Werner. . . . Fred is happy and going to have them bound in with the book."[22] Fred Werner still had some of these illustrations more than half a century later. Others similar to the one reproduced in figure 14 are in Churchill's scrapbook. In a letter of April 16, 1890, Feininger identified Werner to Churchill as "an Australian whom I live with and whom I like very much . . . [he] is studying music and can play beautifully on the piano." In a letter to the author dated July 4, 1958, Mr. Werner recalled:

> We read books, Churchill and other friends would take turns to read aloud. *The Ship of 49* by Bret Harte was a great favourite. I have kept a lot of scraps and sketches which Leo threw into the wastepaper basket; and am enclosing a few, which may be of interest.

Besides their interest in the visual arts, Feininger, Churchill, and Werner also shared a love for literature and music. Although Feininger had given up music as a profession, he continued to play the violin, piano, and harmonium, and composed as well. One of his more acomplished works was published and performed many years later in 1922, while he was living in Weimar.[23] Werner often played Bach for Feininger on the organ of a neighborhood synagogue in Berlin; these performances left an indelible impression on Feininger and strengthened his passion for the fugue, so evident in his later paintings.

The pen drawings to Harte's story, which are washed in purplish ink, benefit from Feininger's expert knowledge of boats and from his earlier acquired skill in rendering them in full detail. Among the drawings which Mr. Werner preserved are three which show a ship moored out of water and serving as a home. Dramatically lit by a single lantern, it stands against a nocturnal sky. The dates on these drawings demonstrate that illustrations for the story occupied Feininger for several months. One of them is inscribed *Frontispiece Feininger 90*. In it, a wooden stepladder is propped against the ship; the ground is littered with a barrel and other objects. The title *A Ship of 49* is decoratively lettered in red and black, the "A" gleaming mysteriously in the light shed by the lantern. (There is a photograph of a less successful version of this title. page in Churchill's scrapbook that offers proof of the care which Feininger bestowed even on casual work.) The other two drawings are less dark and sinister in mood. One, inscribed and signed by Feininger *Original November 1889,* is a view of the boat from the prow. The third and largest, labeled *Skizze Feininger 89,* is the earliest and most closely follows the story—for instance, it is the only one with such details as the name of the boat "Pontiac, Marseilles." It illustrates perfectly the passage:

Between three and four in the morning the clouds broke over the Pontiac, and the moon riding high picked out in black and silver the long bulk that lay cradled between the iron shells of warehouses and the wooden frames of tenement on either side. . . . So peaceful and motionless she lay that she might have been some petrification of a past age now first exhumed and laid bare to the cold light of the stars.

Feininger fell wholeheartedly into the mood of the story, which tells of a once proud old brig, with a treasure of counterfeit coin hidden somewhere inside her, now ignominiously serving out her days on land as a dwelling for quaint characters. Throughout the story the ship is the leading character, and Feininger was far more successful in rendering it than in his attempts to bring some of its residents to life.

Mr. Werner also saved three Feininger illustrations for Dante's *Inferno,* which are from the same period as these drawings for the Harte story and in a similar style. Landscapes of Hell with forbidding rocks, they are reminiscent of Gustave Dóre's celebrated illustrations in their dramatic chiaroscuro.

Two clippings of fantastic watercolor cartoons in Churchill's scrapbook are of even greater interest, since they foretell Feininger's later development. One shows the artist's vision of Friedrich Strasse in Berlin and is signed *L. Feininger 2000;* the other is of fantastic flying apparatus.[24] Both are examples of half-serious, half-humorous science fiction illustrations. Feininger designed them for a special student edition of the magazine *Festzeitung* in the form of a mock newspaper of 2000 A.D. The publication was distributed at the Artist's Ball held in the Berlin Philharmonic Hall on January 15, 1892.

Friedrich Strasse is an astonishing prophecy. In this watercolor, skyscrapers shoot up on both sides of the street, forming a narrow canyon bridged by viaducts and overpasses, while a dirigible sails by overhead. This vision of the young art student, anticipating his later paintings of viaducts, was no doubt stimulated in part by the Jules Verne novels he read so avidly throughout his youth. He wrote Churchill from Liège on October 7, 1890: ". . . have devoured several splendidly illustrated books of Jules Verne[25] illustrated principally by 'Riou' a french artist. . . . those drawings are fantastic and just in my taste." The cartoon also reflects Feininger's childhood memories of the crowded avenues of buildings in old New York, and of the high and narrow footbridges that spanned the railroad tracks near his home.

The second watercolor cartoon, also signed *Feininger 2000*, though artistically less successful, is almost uncanny as a prediction of space travel.

Picture and text tell of a catastrophe which befalls the "Mars Express," a rocketship made up of discs and rotating screws which crashes into another space craft, a kind of rocketship-helicopter called an "Ozonschweber" [ozone-floater]. The caption relates the occurrence in the following way:

The "Mars Express" which has left Berlin at 6 A.M. crashed during the night into the airplane "Ozonschweber" No. 27-114 at a speed of 250 kilometers. Terrible catastrophe! Details are completely lacking up to now. We are indebted for the news and photos to the Luna-Berlin-Air-Observation-Tower. The vehicle is still falling at the moment and can be expected here tomorrow morning at 1 minute and 37 seconds after 4 o'clock. With all probability it will fall into the Havel river.

(Remark by the Editor: We state that such accidents occur much too often in the narrow traffic channel between the two planets the earth and the moon.)

On January 12, 1892, Feininger had announced his desire to

go to Paris with characteristic youthful emphasis: "Next year I go to Paris, or if my people won't hear of it, I'll elope. I have decided to wait until September and earn in the meantime all I can and then, having necessary funds, to go to Paris." A month later, on February 17, Feininger wrote to Churchill that he found "nude study at the Academy dissatisfactory."

His plans materialized in November of the same year when he arrived in Paris to study life drawing at Colarossi, a popular private art school with semi-academic standing.

A letter to Churchill on May 7, 1893, written from the Rue Campagne Première, provides only scanty information about Feininger's first stay in Paris:

I have been here 6 months—since 4th November 1892, and in 8 or 10 days leave for Berlin whither I must go to earn more plunks (return in October). My stay has been wonderfully beneficial to me! wonderfully . . . the only time I have ever been seriously at work and I have been happy in my work.

Shortly after his return—on June 24, 1893—he wrote from Berlin W, Schillstrasse 167:

The French penwork is superb, so is L. L'Hermitte's charcoal work. I never saw an original Monet. I think that as far as a sculptor, who merely rough-hews a statue, however splendid the blocked proportions, can be called great, so far can Monet be called the same.

This qualified praise was a response to Churchill's recommendation of Monet's work. From the time of his first stay in Paris and all through his later life, Churchill was an enthusiastic admirer of Monet. Feininger's interest in French art at that time seems less advanced than his friend's—a situation that was later reversed.

While in Paris Feininger concentrated on studying the human figure in order to provide a foundation for his pen drawings. It does not seem odd that he mentioned Léon L'Hermitte's charcoal drawings when we consider the technical interest in charcoals he had acquired at the Berlin Academy. From Berlin he had sent Churchill charcoal studies of an ear and of Napoleon's death mask in a mixed technique (in Churchill's scrapbook; see also letters of July 31 and October 6, 1891) and had written,

> I work very freely with coal—getting the principal characteristic lines in first and always rubbing with my fingers and a medium-sized bristly brush to get the tones, after which I model a good deal with a pointed piece of charcoal and draw with hard, sharp charcoal. Always have a soft rubber or bread.

The somewhat melodramatic social consciousness of L'Hermitte's work might also have appealed to him; L'Hermitte's then-famous *Death of the Woodchopper* is similar to Feininger's composition *Death and the Miser* (Detroit scrapbook).

In June of 1893, after Feininger returned to Berlin, now his permanent home, he and Churchill wrote to each other much less frequently. The artistic aims of the two friends seem to have diverged more and more. Both men entered into the serious struggle of establishing themselves in their chosen professions, Churchill as a college art teacher in the United States, Feininger as a cartoonist and illustrator in Berlin. Feininger's next letter to Churchill was written ten months later (April 6, 1894), still from the same Berlin address, Schillstrasse 16: "I've had a number of drawings accepted by Harper and Brothers in January and a few days ago a second batch were accepted."

The drawings must be the ones for "How Fritz Became a Wizard," a children's story written by John Kendrick Bangs for *Harper's Young People* and published in the issue of October 2, 1894. Two of the originals in pen, ink, and wash are preserved in the Library of Congress. One has the caption *The Little Fellow Mused Oft and Long Thereon;* Feininger sent a tracing of it signed F. 1894 to Churchill, who preserved it in his scrapbook. The second is entitled *It Nearly Blinded Him.* The drawing and humor both anticipate Feininger's cartoons for the *Chicago Sunday Tribune.*

Bangs commissioned illustrations for two further stories, "A Birthday Party in Topsyturvydom" and "The Old Settler at Zurich," both of which also appeared in *Harper's Young People*.[26] He might have selected Feininger, who was virtually unknown in America, because two of the stories took place in a German-speaking fairy-tale country that must have resembled Feininger's childhood image of his parents' homeland. The setting of "How Fritz Became a Wizard" is "Schnitzelhammerstein-on-the-Zugwitz," whose mayor is "Hans Pumpernickel." For the story laid in Zurich, Feininger made an illustration of some musicians in old-fashioned clothes performing a string trio; the caption reads *The Three Men Fiddled Away with All Their Strength*. This scene and its inherent humor doubtless derived from Feininger's memories of home concerts performed by his father with friends of the family.

A careful pencil tracing of the same scene dated April 2, 1894, has been preserved in Kortheuer's scrapbook (fig. 15). The tracing indicates the great care that Feininger bestowed on details of eighteenth-century costumes, furniture, and musical instruments. This devotion to detail is evident in all his genre studies set in the past and is invariably joined with a highly individual fantasy and humor (see the pen drawing *Old Woman with Baby* dated Berlin, 1894, fig. 16). There are more illustrations of jolly topers and elderly men sitting about smoking or taking snuff and amusing themselves in tavern camaraderie. The style seems more indebted to E. A. Abbey's illustrations of Tudor and Shakespearean scenes for *Harper's Magazine* than to Vogel's fairy-tale renderings of the German middle ages in the Munich *Fliegende Blätter*. The captions are in "olde English": *Ye Fyddler, Ye Lyttle Gardener, Ye Pinche of Snuffe*.

Feininger drew such types as late as 1901, when he made *Ye Learned Apothecary*, now in the collection of Mrs. Julia Feininger. It is carefully executed in pencil, Chinese white and brownish wash (fig. 17). It shows the learned man balancing a tiny mortarboard on his extremely high forehead and carrying a huge bottle marked with skull and crossbones. A comparison with Feininger's *Spooks Wearing Mortar Boards* (in the possession of Mrs. Julia Feininger) from the last year of his life demonstrates the

15. Pencil tracing of illustration for *Harper's Young People*. 1894.

16. *Old Woman with Child.*
Pen illustration intended for
Harper's Young People. 1894.

difference between still conventional cartoon humor and free artistic fantasy.

Feininger's close observation of the architectural features of Belgian towns may have been responsible for the authenticity of the drawings of 1894, with details like the Dutch door and carved beams of a late Gothic house in the drawing *The Mysterious Messenger.* Originals or tracings of many of these drawings, all intended for *Harper's,* are in Kortheuer's scrapbook.

In the same letter in which Feininger informed Churchill of his success with *Harper's,* he outlined more fully than ever before his aims as illustrator and caricaturist.

Of course book-illustration is my aim and *zwar* [what is more] for the present, at least, illustrations of fantastic subjects as: Fairy Stories, *Nonsense* stories (I hear old Al groan at this) and Children's Books; I find in this field everything to call out my powers and feel happy in my work; which is the *Hauptsache* [main thing] . . . I think without pride or vanity that I may claim to be alone in my line of work in America.

Feininger's next letter (June 22, 1894) elaborated on the specifically American character of his style by contrasting it with that of the most famous German illustrators of fairy tales, Ludwig Richter and Hermann Vogel. Ludwig Richter, the amiable representative of late Romanticism, "the favorite of the German home," had been dead for ten years at the time that Feininger wrote about him. Hermann Vogel, fifty-three years younger than Richter, continued the Dresden line of romantic illustration in a more decorative yet more superficial and prettified manner. Vogel's illustrations for *Grimm's Fairy Tales* and other works were then appearing in books and in the humor magazine *Fliegende Blätter.* Feininger wrote:

You know that although there are in Germany some splendid fairy-tale illustrators: Hermann Vogel, Richter, etc., yet none of them have paid much [attention] to anything more than the decorative and glamorous part of fairy- or wonder Tale depiction. . . . I get on a distinctly different, very individual, *un*-traditional mis-

17. *Ye Learned Apothecary.* Pencil, watercolor, opaque white. 1901.

sion, such as is after all, *the only thing to do* where the country
for which I work and always mean to work (America) is itself
in these matters so little traditional. . . . I mean to assure the
position of the *Nonsense*-Story, which title does not preclude the
possibility of its containing pure humor, feeling etc., by any
means! . . . I have an idea for an entire book, a series of quaint
chronicles, to be written and illustrated by myself. . . .

The last sentence is a prophecy of the cartoons which appeared
more than ten years later in the *Chicago Sunday Tribune.* Feininger at twenty-three was already quite sure of himself and informed his friend that he was "at liberty as to the choice of subjects
and having them accepted so far, invariably."

In 1894 Feininger became increasingly aware of his mission:
the introduction of a very personal, whimsical, and fantastic cartoon style into the illustration of American children's books. In
the same year he resumed the correspondence with Kortheuer.
These letters to Kortheuer are full of Feininger's hopes of working for *Harper's* and other American publishing houses and, ultimately, returning to America. He felt that every year spent in
Europe increased his involvement with European culture in general, and with German culture in particular. He welcomed the
commission from *Harper's* because he hoped that his work for
them would strengthen his ties to America. On January 8, 1894
he wrote Kortheuer from Berlin:

At times it seems impossible to me that I should ever have
been in America, and yet I assure you, too, that I have lost none
of my American appearance[27] by 'contamination' with Germans
for 6½ years.
I am yearly expecting to be back in New York, but somehow
it doesn't happen. It has been a great and splendid thing for me
to be able to study in Germany and France. (I was 7 months in
Paris last Winter and Spring) and I have become more attached
to old-world refinement and influences than I possibly can realize,
until they are once out of my grasp.
. . . Once known to a few standard publishing houses in
America my chances of earning a living from the time of my arrival
in America are tenfold increased.

I still (and shall always) take the warmest interest in locomotives, ships, and all inventions. I sometimes feel that [I could] have been very content in my calling [had] my calling been that of Machinist or shipbuilder.

I made a little model of a Brigantine this Summer and it hangs in my room from the ceiling.

A photograph in the possession of Mrs. Julia Feininger shows Leo with the brigantine (fig. 18). A letter of February 27, 1894 explained that it is a reproduction of a seventeenth-century ship and that Feininger tried to get "the ancient rig and model correct."

In the same letter Feininger announced that from time to time he would send Kortheuer the *Fliegende Blätter* in which Adolf Oberländer's work[28] interested him most; in return Kortheuer would send journals such as *Engineering Magazine* (with articles on locomotives, bridge-building, and electric motors), *Munsey's Magazine, Cosmopolitan,* and the Christmas number of *Scribner's.* Next to discussions about progress in American mechanical and electrical engineering (Kortheuer's specialty), Feininger loved to engage his friend in an evaluation of the comparative merits of American and German illustration and cartooning.

On the occasion of sending Kortheuer issues of the *Fliegende Blätter* he said: "The paper is a very fine publication in its humor and in the lead for refined genuinity, and the drawing sometimes just splendid. It beats any of our American humor papers when it is at its best." And again in praise of the *Fliegende Blätter* on the next postcard of March 10, 1894:

We have nothing like them in America (I mean in their style or as good) although Frost[29] and Opper [the creator of "Happy Hooligan"][30] are just as fine in a *different* branch of humor. Frost is the king of American illustrators of humorous subjects. Howard Pyle, E. A. Abbey, W. T. Smedley, C. S. Reinhardt are the "big ones."

Other illustrators mentioned in the correspondence beside these and the earlier discussed "Zim" are: Charles Dana Gibson, Peter Newell, Ch. H. Johnson (who worked chiefly for *Truth*), Brennan and Blum.

18. Feininger with brigantine. 1894.

At this time Feininger's cartoon style was almost completely devoid of Busch's influence and was coming closer to that of Frost (see Frost's cartoon "The Perennial Drama of the American Quest for Culture in Europe" [1878]).[31] Among the illustrators of this period, only Peter Newell (1862–1924), with his decidedly whimsical view of this world of men, animals and things,[32] is akin to Feininger's fantastic humor. Newell also illustrated many stories by J. K. Bangs of *Harper's Young People.* Feininger summed up his opinion of these two artists:

> The two humorous artists I most admire: Frost and Peter Newell, the latter a most talented, promising (young?) fellow whose work began to appear not much longer than a year ago.[33]

He most clearly expressed his aims as an illustrator in a long letter to Kortheuer on April 2, 1894.

> I live half of the time in a world of my own creation, as does almost every imaginative artist, and my interests are centering themselves into a focus upon matters most immediately in connexion with my present and eventual needs. I had great encouragement from Harper and Brothers in New York and sold some more works to them a few days ago. They wrote me a cordial letter (for a business letter) soliciting the further sending of all sort of fanciful sketches of 'fairies, gnomes, goblins' etc., which is just what I am working for. . . . Am devoting all my work to developing a field of illustration in which I shall feel myself contented, collecting materials from museums and libraries for the same and making all sorts of *Nature Studien* of objects I can use in it. . . . I become daily more impressed with the fact that I can do more good in America than here and that my country has the first right to my services, I am just thinking now of the one thing: how to better the class of juvenile illustrated works and periodicals in America. There are so few artists who have the 'gemueth' [temperament] to patiently devote themselves to this work. . . . My drawings for Harper's are 'slightly' caricatured but in a way which, I flatter myself, does not cause repulsion, but only adds to the vividness of the characterization. And the secret of their *not* impressing one as being deformed, is because they are obviously represented as being 'pygmies' or a little race of (principally) dutch and 'olde Englishe.'

The turning-point of Feininger's career as a cartoonist was reached in 1894 when he began to work for *Ulk*, the humorous Sunday supplement of the liberal and occasionally leftist *Berliner Tageblatt* (Berlin Daily News). The *Tageblatt*, which had the largest circulation of any Berlin newspaper at that time, made Feininger so well-known that other Berlin humor magazines began to vie with each other to engage him as a contributor. They were: the politically more neutral *Lustige Blätter* (*The Jolly Sheets*), *Berliner Illustrierte Zeitung* (Berlin Illustrated Magazine), *Sporthumor, Der Wahre Jacob* (*The Real Jacob*—a slang expression equivalent to 'the real McCoy'), *Narrenschiff* (*Ship of Fools*), and its special issue, *Narrenrad* (*Wheel of Fools*).

Narrenschiff was the most ambitious and sophisticated of these magazines in content and art work, fully living up to Sebastian Brant's satirical masterpiece of the same name. *Narrenrad*, which appeared only once, gave Feininger, the cycling enthusiast who specialized in bike humor at this time, a wonderful opportunity to show his ability. In the cover of an 1898 issue of *Narrenschiff* called "Two Bicyclists" (fig. 30), he had already shown his kinship with Brant's spirit by giving to the two contrasting characters, the top-hatted Sunday biker and the more professionally garbed racer, the medieval fool's cap and bells.

The need to earn quick money soon forced Feininger to rely more and more on the German market, though he continued to send drawings to *Harper's* and the Century Company (publishers of *St. Nicholas* magazine) in New York. In spite of his desire to go to New York—a desire that became particularly strong when he was depressed—personal involvements as well as sickness and death in his family kept him in Berlin. On October 1, 1897, he became a staff member of *Ulk*, at a handsome salary. (Before this, as a contributing artist, he had been paid only for those drawings which *Ulk* accepted.) The contract was terminated four months later, on February 1, 1898, but by then Feininger's position as one of the leading Berlin illustrators was assured and he never again lacked work.

Feininger always felt that his cartoons for the Berlin humor magazines were important in his development as an artist. Years later he wrote to Dr. Eysler, the publisher of *Lustige Blätter:*

I am far from underestimating in my development the very important years which I spent as a draftsman for "Funny Papers"—on the contrary! They were the only means to discipline myself. . . .[34]

Lux Feininger gives a penetrating evaluation of his father's activity as a caricaturist:

A discussion of Lyonel Feininger's paintings demands mention of his early days as an illustrator and cartoonist. My father always insisted on the inestimable value which the ten years or so of his purely drawing period had for him. Working in the graphic media of linecut and lithograph to the specification of dimension, subject matter (all too often some nauseating 'punch line') and time, provided exactly that kind of obstacle course, in which an inferior talent might exhaust himself. My father however drew strength from it. Not only the invention of designs compositionally strong and effective, but the study of the million aspects of reality—to be drawn only from nature—seems to have inspired him with an almost ecstatic fervor. Effects of light, the textural value of the city, landscape in cobblestone pavement, towering brick walls, the waves of the canals intersecting the city of Berlin, the construction of mechanical devices, notably ships, sail and steam, railroads, bicycles quite particularly; the effect of costume on the human figure; the physiognomic structure of faces. The papers he worked for were all more or less radical in policy and wreaked weekly havoc on members of the Reichstag, of the cabinet and, above all, the Military. All this called for endless drawing which seemed (in retrospect) to have been done, as one might say, at a canter. If the material were not almost totally unavailable today, a study of the portraiture alone, necessary to persiflage and caricature hundreds of statesmen and public figures of Germany, France, England, Russia, Japan, America, Italy, Austria, together with their uniforms and insignia, orders and decorations, whiskers, helmets, plumed hats, liveries of flunkies, carriages and horses, palaces and mistresses would provide a theme for a book. But all this rich subject matter would be insignificant without the compositional arrangement full or half page, the design of black and white, with inexhaustible resources of textural grays, almost invariably prepared for the engraver by the artist himself, for black and white or color lithography. One of the papers my father worked for had four-color reproduction, and a very considerable formal knowledge of composition was accumulated through making the color separation submitted with the complete art work at press time.[35]

Feininger drew hundreds of cartoons for Berlin newspapers and magazines during the decade from 1897 to 1907. The subjects of these cartoons fall into several categories: Germany's foreign and domestic policies, social satire, the visual and literary arts, transportation, mechanical devices, ghosts and fantasy. The political cartoons comprise the most numerous category. In this category especially, Feininger is a champion of all liberal causes. Before he had worked for *Ulk,* Feininger had shown relatively little interest in internal or external politics, though his descent from a family of "48 refugees" destined him to become a "liberal." The news that the German crown prince Friedrich, on whom the German liberals had set all their hopes, was dying of cancer of the throat is mentioned to Kortheuer (Feb. 27, 1888). Ten years later, he referred to the Dreyfus affair as "the greatest social calamity of the century" (Jan. 30, 1898).

As far as American politics were concerned, he was a Lincolnian Republican, in spite of his father's and grandfather's ties to the South; but he adds in this letter of December 6, 1894 to Kortheuer: "I don't think it can possibly make much difference what I am, as I know as good as nothing about politics, and do not vote either, though I hope to become a staunch American citizen before long." The victories of the United States Navy in the Spanish American War "thrilled" him (Kortheuer letter May 3, 1898).

Among his colleagues at *Ulk,* it was especially Siegmar Mehring who had a decisive influence on Feininger's political thinking. Feininger was always a welcome guest at Mehring's home. In his book *Notorious Painting (Verrufene Malerei),*[36] Mehring's son

69

Walter recalls Feininger's "Mephistophelean caricatures of heads of statesmen and politicians, which hung above my father's writing desk together with a fat 'Kobold baby' in watercolor sucking his big toe (for which I posed)."[37] Fig. 19 reproduces a cartoon of a staff meeting at *Ulk* which Feininger sent Kortheuer. The editor R. Schmidt-Cabanis presides, holding a huge pair of scissors like a mighty sword. Feininger identifies the others for Kortheuer —left to right: Gehrke, Manzel, the political cartoonist and former sculptor who had brought Feininger to *Ulk,* the previously mentioned Siegmar Mehring, and F. Engel. Behind the massive Schmidt-Cabanis stands Leo, tall and lanky, with pointed nose, chin, and moustache. Feininger also portrayed himself in two other sequences of the cartoon—throwing the chief's ideas on paper and pouring color on it. The result of this not-too-happy teamwork appears in the last cartoon and resembles a child's drawing. The whole bears the ironical title *Fame.*

Related in subject matter is a pen drawing *Editorial Staff and Prosecuting Attorney (Redaktion und Staatsanwalt)* which Feininger did in 1898 for *Narrenschiff* (fig. 20).[38] It shows in the top drawing the Editor-in-Chief, the Bookseller, the Publisher and the Designer (Zeichner) in a conference around a table. The designer, in whom Feininger has caricatured himself stylishly dressed and with a pince-nez on his nose, is displaying his characters: a diplomat and a king, both puppet-sized. Other questionable characters such as a policeman, a radical socialist ("Sozi"), and a ridiculous-looking officer have been already discarded and thrown into a box. The bottom drawing shows Feininger again, now himself reduced to the size of a tiny puppet, whom the Prosecuting Attorney (Der Herr Staatsanwalt) drops into a roofless replica of Plötzensee Penitentiary, the notorious prison for the Berlin district. His colleagues are next; they still remain firmly grasped in the enormous hand of the law. A helmeted police sergeant looks on with an expression of stupid approval.

For the few cartoons in which the idea or text was not supplied by the editor, as in the previously discussed example, Feininger

Beilage

Der Ruhm.

Auf mich gab Niemand Acht
　　In all' der Menschen Zahl,
Da habe ich gemacht
'ne große Dummheit 'mal.
Im Blatt stand ich gedruckt
Als neu'ste Sensation,
Und eh' ich noch gemuckt,
Traf mich das Schicksal schon.

Man trug mich
　　meuchlings hin
Zur Zeichner-Konferenz
Und kitzelte mich in
Satyrischer Tendenz.

Man fragte mich
erst nicht
Und schmiß mich
auf's Papier

Und warf in mein
Gesicht
'nen Topf voll
Farbe mir.

Man ätzte
mich —
man schob
Mich in die
Presse dann:

So wurde ich —
　　Gottlob,
Ein sehr
berühmter
Mann.

19. *Fame* (*Der Ruhm*). Panel cartoon for *Ulk*. Circa 1898.

was able to make a satirical point through his drawings alone. In one series of cartoons he ridiculed the depravity of the dueling fraternities (fig. 21).[39] Here he also employed a child's drawing style which Oberländer had introduced into the German humor magazines. The humor of these drawings is similar to that of the *Concerts* of Feininger's boyhood. But what had been the natural expression of an imagination which had not yet mastered the technical means of expression was now a conscious, quite sophisticated instrument of satirical humor.

Feininger's magazine work in Germany did not often give him an opportunity for pure humor or fantasy. This talent he hoped to display in the nonsense stories he planned to write and illustrate for the American magazines. He wanted to give his cartoons an individual style and a flavor which the German public and critics considered typically American, and decided that he could best accomplish this in his whimsical treatment of mechanical gadgets and weird contraptions.

Emil Preetorius, the outstanding artist, book illustrator, stage designer, and early champion of the "Biedermeier Revival," summed up his impressions of Feininger's early cartoon work:

These cartoons possessed a ghostly quality full of contrasts. They were old-fashioned and romantic, yet at the same time ultra-modern and technological. Great sensitivity was fused with an acid sharpness in a peculiar and impressive mixture.[40]

Feininger became an early admirer of flying apparatus. It is possible that his brother-in-law Arthur Berson, a famous balloonist and meteorologist, contributed to this interest. Feininger wrote about him (on January 8, 1894) to Kortheuer:

When the flying machine comes, I suppose man will be, for a short time, satisfied speaking of flying machines. My sister's intended husband is a regular celebrity, having made some remarkable ascensions together with a Prussian artillery officer. . . . My future brother-in-law is a real genius, a regular encyclopedia of scientific knowledge.[41]

Im „Taxameter" steigt des Kneipfuchs' „flüssige Säule" —

21. Carousing fraternity-student.
Pen cartoon for *Ulk.* 1895.

20. *Editorial Staff and Prosecuting Attorney*
    (*Redaktion und Staatsanwalt*).
    Pen cartoon for *Narrenschiff.* 1898.

A cartoon in Churchill's scrapbook published in *Ulk* on August 23, 1895, is called *How to Make Pianos Harmless* (fig. 22). The pianos are suspended from balloons and are carried by them to a considerable height over the town. Virtuosi with the famous "Liszt-mane" and gestures can now bang *a furioso* on their concert-grands while the female sex can hammer wildly on the upright or can play endless four-hand-scales. Their only connection with the earth is by telephone wire ending in earphones so that music teachers as well as intrepid enthusiasts may not be robbed of their pleasure. On another copy of this cartoon which he sent to Kortheuer there is a pencilled question: "Doesn't this recall some of our old 'Concert' Drawings?" Feininger was referring to the particular kind of humor involving musical instruments rather than to the style; but it is interesting that he was aware of the continuity of his fantasy from the early sketches to the drawings for *Ulk*. He was encouraged to imagine flying machines and other "fantastic" means of transportation by the turn-of-the-century penchant for speculation about the future inventions of mankind. His talent for prophecy (*Friedrich Strasse in Berlin* was an early example) earned him the post on *Ulk*. His cartoons of *Means of Transportation in the Future*—fantastic airplanes and ghostly mail carriers—appeared in the issue of July 5, 1895; Feininger sent the cartoons to Kortheuer with the notation, "Some of my oldest work for *Ulk*."

This was the time of struggle between the horse-drawn carriage and that new invention, the electric streetcar. Feininger drew the *Electric Horse* (fig. 23) as a modernized Saurian creature spewing forth bolts of lightning and gleaming incandescently. He also drew a streetcar-caused traffic jam on the Lützowplatz, one of Berlin's busiest squares. He solved the pedestrian problem by having the pedestrians walk over the jam on the telephone wires.

Among Feininger's wittiest conceptions of the world to come are the two reproduced in figs. 24 and 25. They appeared in *Ulk* without captions. In the first, all types of boats have been converted to airplanes that rise from the Berlin canals and fly between

74

22. *How to Make Pianos Harmless* (*Unschädlichmachung der Klaviere*). Color cartoon for *Ulk*. Circa 1895.

Das elektrische Pferd.

23. *The Electric Horse (Das elektrische Pferd).*
Color cartoon for *Ulk.* Circa 1894.

24. Navigation problems of air-borne canal traffic.
Color cartoon for *Ulk.* Circa 1896.

25. "Deutschmeer, D-e-u-t-schmeer, ü-ü-ber Alles!" *leo feininger.* *Ulk Marinier.* Pen cartoon for *Ulk.* 1896.

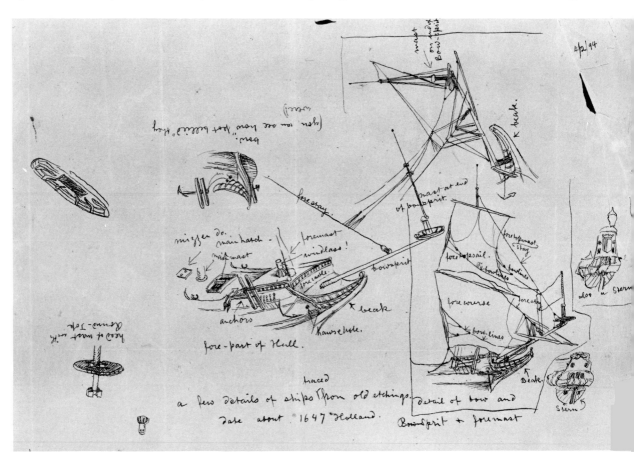

the "Sieges-Allee" and the neo-Gothic city hall, and yet are unable to avoid traffic accidents. So progress, which has conquered the kingdom of the air, has not changed anything. In the second, a pen and ink drawing which occupied a double-page spread, boats are again central. Berlin is shown under water with its inhabitants forced to take to the boats; it is signed *leo feininger Ulk Marinier* (sic!) *1896*. It is certainly Feininger's most important work as a cartoonist for *Ulk,* since in both content and style it is prophetic of his later work as etcher and painter. It is a link in the chain which extended from his sophisticated children's-scrawl manner to the "Einfinger" etchings of 1911 and anticipated the grotesque letterheads which he made for his son Laurence in 1951 (fig. 49). The drawing is crowded with minutely rendered details. The gas lantern rising above the water has become the home of a sea dragon, whose tail winds around it. Clustered around the lantern are some of Feininger's chief political targets: there is the policeman, now regulating traffic on a sea monster; the Minister of Finance von Miquel with the *Steuer Rochen* [tax sting ray]; the Kaiser's luxury yacht *Aegir* reduced to the size of a rowboat, and without the Kaiser; a school-and-church boat with men overboard; the Imperial Chancellery with its files. The lives of the little men, the average Berlin burghers, go on as though nothing had happened—as usual, they sing, drink, and play cards in various boats. Their favorite cigar stores, hat shops, and honkytonks are not forgotten. The artist lives in the crow's-nest of the most majestic ship. Under him a maiden sings "German Sea, German Sea above Everything" (*Deutschmeer, Deutschmeer über alles*).

In this cartoon Feininger satirized the Kaiser's plan to build a large fleet which could challenge England. Two years later, in 1898, "The First Law Concerning the Navy" (Erstes Flottengesetz) had been accepted by the Reichstag and subsequently the superpatriotic "Association for Support of the Navy" (Flottenverein) had been founded. The second "Flottengesetz" (1902) asked for a still larger appropriation and was an attempt to build up the

26. Details of old ships traced from etchings. 1894.

27. *Marine*. Etching. 1911.

rapidly growing navy to the point at which even the strongest adversary would suffer certain defeat if he dared a naval attack. The Kaiser with his usual tactlessness and braggadocio trumpeted: "Germany's future lies on the water!" ("Deutschlands Zukunft liegt auf dem Wasser.") These words, addressed to Germany but meant for England, announced that only a great navy could guarantee Germany's trade and colonial expansion. But Feininger rightly sensed in the ambiguous and ominous pronouncement the prophecy of a deluge which would inundate and destroy German life. He uses the phrase of the Emperor word for word as caption for another two-color cartoon which appeared 1905 in *Ulk*.[42]

Although the first drawing of 1896 is fanciful, it displays a most exact knowledge of boats of all kinds and periods. The ship with the crow's-nest has the carved prow of a seventeenth-century warship, rendered with an exactness reflecting Feininger's patient study of such details in old prints at the marine museums of Paris and Berlin. He also used the results of his researches for the model boats with which he decorated his rooms. One of the study sheets with such original pen drawings was sent to Kortheuer (fig. 26). Dated April 2, 1894, it is covered with expert and elegant renderings of parts of old ships; Feininger wrote on it, "Traced from old etchings, dated about 1647 Holland." Such studies were kept for reference and were used in later works such as the 1911 etching *Marine* (fig. 27).

Feininger was acidly sharp in the cartoons dealing with the German class and police state. The anti-Junker American artist mocked the servility of the "Untertan" (German subjects) in a cartoon published around 1910 in *Der Wahre Jacob*. Two state's attorneys, one dressed in his official robes, the other sporting dueling scars, bow their heads before "His Excellency," who, without paying the least attention to them, gargles while cleaning his teeth. Behind the mighty man a lackey in rich livery holding a silver washbowl and a towel stands at attention.[43] In a cartoon showing Feininger's proposal for a monument to Bismarck (*Ulk*, October 22, 1897), to whom absurdly elaborate memorials had already been erected from one end of Germany to the other, he puts the Iron Chancellor in armor on a bicycle and decorates the pedestal with savage caricatures of the leaders of the conservative clique; Feininger sent a clipping of this cartoon to Churchill. The original drawing for a cartoon ridiculing the Berlin police is preserved in the Archives of American Art, Detroit, Michigan. It shows two "custodians of order" in their silver-braided blue uniforms, wearing spiked helmets (Pickelhauben) and white gloves. They command the chickens, directing them where to lay their eggs. The often-caricatured policeman stands as a symbol of Feininger's fight against reaction, suppression, and all that was rotten in Imperial Germany. Even the Kaiser was not exempt from Feininger's barbs: he appears as a giant in shining guardsman's uniform before the "temple of peace," from which he expels the merchants trading in that rare article, world peace.[44]

Feininger opposed the ultra-nationalism and anti-Semitism of the court cleric Adolf Stöcker and his bigoted clique in a cartoon depicting them as bickering horses pulling the Victory Chariot of conservatism off the Brandenburg Gate (fig. 28). He also ridiculed the opportunism of the Minister of Finance Johannes von Miquel, who betrayed the liberalism of his youth for political advancement and a patent of nobility. Neither Postmaster-General Stephan nor the Third Chancellor of Germany, well-meaning but ancient Prince Chlodwig von Hohenlohe-Schillingsfürst, was safe from Feininger's attacks. The privileges of the nobility, of the officer class, and of the students belonging to exclusive fraternities were constantly under his fire.

In foreign policy, as we have already seen in his handling of the Kaiser's naval megalomania, Feininger displayed a most belligerent sharpness against the ruler as well as against the Reichschancellors who followed in rapid succession the "Fall of Bismarck" in 1890. Though the next two decades of European history were rather peaceful, there were marginal wars in Asia and Africa and constant disturbances on the fringe of Europe: the Balkans.

The Chinese Boxers rebelled in 1900 against white exploitation,

28. *Conservative Disunity* (*Konservative Veruneinigung*). Cover illustration for *Ulk*. 1897.

and the Japanese defeated the Russians spectacularly in a relatively short war (1904–5). In South Africa the valiant resistance of the Boers was finally crushed by the might of the British Empire (1899–1902). Royal assassinations and the creation of new thrones and their overthrow, as a result of rivalry between the great powers, Austria–Germany and Russia, were common occurrences in the Balkans, "Europe's Powderkeg."

Feininger was skeptical of Russian aims in the Dardanelles and of Russian flirtation with the French. He showed contempt for the vice-ridden regime of Sultan Abdul Hamid, "the sick man of Europe," as well as for the great European powers, which were only too eager to carve up Turkey or at least carry off some pieces such as Crete, which in Feininger's cartoons became literally a bone of contention.

Together with the majority of the German people, Feininger sided with the Boers in their fight against Britain. A cover illustration done by Feininger for *Lustige Blätter* during the Boer War (fig. 29) depicts a condemned Boer commandant awaiting execution. When asked by the foppish British officer who holds his death warrant if he has a last wish, the commandant requests gruffly that a fellow Boer be included in the firing squad. "That way I can be sure that at least *one* bullet hits me."

Feininger was also sympathetic to the Chinese, who were potential victims of Western economic and political exploitation under the guise of "modernization." [45] "Zopf ab!" ("Off with the Pigtail!") was the battle cry of the exploiters. A book by that name —"*Zopf ab*"—was issued by the publishers of *Lustige Blätter* (Dr. Eysler and Company, Berlin) with the subtitle: *Die Chinesiche Affaire in der Karikatur aller Völker* (*The Chinese Affair in the Cartoons of All Peoples*). Feininger designed its cover (fig. 31). The publication date is not indicated, but it must have been in one of the first years of the twentieth century. The cover shows not only Feininger's great talent as a designer but also his refined sense of color in the unusual contrast of yellow and blue-gray. The flat, posteresque design and the signature draw their Oriental character

LUSTIGE BLÄTTER

Redaction: ALEX. MOSZKOWSKI.
Dr. L. Wulff.

Verlag der Lustigen Blätter
Dr. Eysler & Co., G. m. b. H.

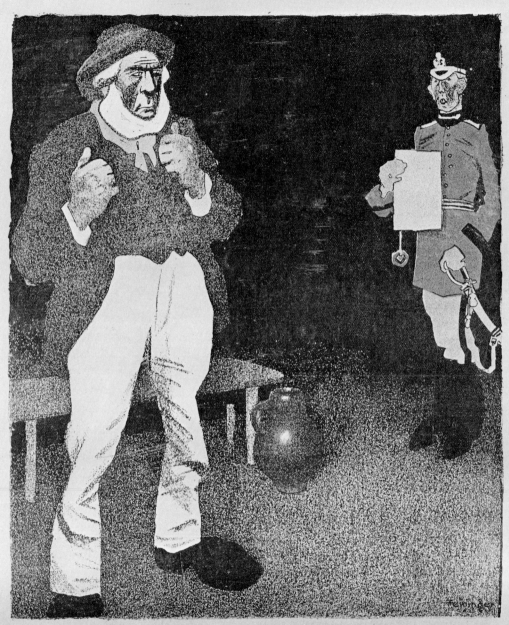

Execution.

— Die Hinrichtung wird morgen von zwölf Hochländer-Scharfschützen an Ihnen vollstreckt werden. Haben Sie noch einen letzten Wunsch zu äussern?

Der verurtheilte Burenkommandant: Ja, könnte nicht vielleicht einer von den gefangenen Buren mitschiessen, damit mich wenigstens Einer trifft?!

29. *Execution.* Cover illustration for *Lustige Blätter*. Circa 1902.

from the Japanese woodcut, an influence quite common in advanced design of this period, but the choice or blending of colors in Feininger's work of that time owes little to Japonism and still less to *Art Nouveau*. It may rather have been the result of Feininger's special feeling for color and its symbolic function. The color in *Blood Rain* (fig. 32) is bloody indeed, although more rosé than deep red, and there is a deliciously macabre contrast of olive green and violet in *Man of the Diluvium* (*Diluvial Mensch*).[46]

Feininger was a master in the orchestral blending of his four favorite colors: olive, violet, blue-gray and rosé. He wrote about color relationships:

Do not think exclusively of the key-stone [which gives the design in contourlines]. The whole [printing process] must be conducted like an orchestra. Only in this way can you achieve the magic integration of the hues and their values with the rich complementing function of shades, textures and blots. Without this integration your work will always remain just a contour-drawing to which color has been added. To utilize to the fullest the potentialities of the technical process of printing is a necessary prerequisite of success in this art.[47]

While the blending of unusual colors enhances the mood quality and through that the message of a cartoon, the distortions in size of figures (elongation as well as shrinking of proportions), crazy angles of architecture and trees, an array of figures and objects along a "shooting diagonal" are the constantly improved means by which Feininger gained most of his strong caricaturistic effects. He was also not above the old standby of the caricaturist to gain ridiculous effects: by exaggerating prominent features of the heads of his victims. The noses of Balkan Kings and of the Turkish Sultan were in this respect delightfully vulnerable.[48]

Since Pieter Bruegel the Elder, contrasts of fat and lean also have been standard devices of the caricaturist. Fox-nosed, top-hatted "Joe" Chamberlain in *Blood Rain* is tall and lean as a beanstalk; "Fat Eddy in Marienbad,"[49] England's Prince of Wales and fashion-ruling playboy, is as round as an overinflated beach ball.

Another of Feininger's favorite targets was Teddy Roosevelt. His toothy, broad grin and walrus moustache appeared frequently in Feininger's cartoons for *Lustige Blätter*[50] and *Ulk.*[51] Feininger comments pictorially on the Western Rancher and Rough Rider's campaign for the presidency in a 1904 cartoon called *The Big Throw (Der grosse Wurf)*, and in *Teddy's Victory Howl (Teddy's Siegesgeheul)* of the same year. Feininger's skepticism concerning the President's self-appointed role as arbiter in world politics and peacemaker was expressed in such cartoons as *Hague Peace Conference, Roosevelt Presiding (Die Friedenskonferenz im Haag unter Roosevelts Vorsitz)* of 1904, and *The New Miracle Working Icon (Das neue wundertätige Heiligenbild)* of 1905, which refers to the President's role as mediator in the Russo-Japanese War.

Feininger's excellent political cartoons were an almost daily task, requiring the most time-consuming research in libraries and archives. The pressure of his work, which he sometimes considered mere drudgery, as well as depressing personal circumstances, led to increasingly greater gaps in the correspondence with his two friends. The summer of 1894 brought an emotional crisis which, as he wrote to Kortheuer,[52] led to "an insane notion of self-destruction." At this time, long, solitary bicycle trips were his distraction. "You must think I am only thinking of bicycling and that there is no other interest for me," he wrote in one of his now brief and infrequent letters to Kortheuer.[53] Another consolation during these difficult years was music. Feininger wrote to Kortheuer that he had bought a fine organ for his "smoky little den," adding "The sweetest hours I know are those spent in the ocean of grand sounds woven in and out through Bach's immortal fugues and chorales."[54]

The correspondence with his other close friend had been totally suspended for almost two years and was only resumed when Feininger learned of the Churchills' approaching visit to Berlin. In a letter from Friedenau on April 30, 1896, Feininger proclaimed to "Al" his position in the world of the Berlin humor magazines:

I am the regular artist on a prominent humorous satirical weekly, just as I used to imagine I would become! And my name is becoming "a power in the land." . . . A high-priest as it were of HUMOR which is the very salt of our daily existence! . . . As fantasie is a very remarkable commodity now-adays, I am doing very well indeed, when you consider that I only commenced 14 months ago to work for German papers. In that year my income, at first about 50 M(arks) a month is now over four times as much, and I have every prospect of earning twice as much again the coming year! There is already the question of my being permanently engaged by the one paper *Ulk* and the salary wouldn't be less than 4,500 M yearly.

These somewhat boastful remarks are understandable coming from a twenty-five-year-old who had established himself so well in so short a time in a foreign land. The fact that he always knew how to joke about himself is one of the charms of these letters. In the foregoing one he called himself "poor fantastic dweller on the negative side of the sublime," and in a letter written two years later (January 29, 1898) he wrote: "One thing is sure: that I shall never set the Thames, the Seine, nor yet the East River afire."

Nevertheless, near the turn of the century the German critics were ranking him among the leading Berlin cartoonists. The once-celebrated Berlin journalist, essayist, novelist and art collector, Georg Hermann, began an evaluation of Feininger in the following way:

The first among the Berlin draftsmen is Lionell Feininger. Though as a native American of German descent he still shows traces of Yankee-dom and Yankee snobbery in his burlesque exaggerations, he has lately created in a style of typically Berlin humor, which is nevertheless his own.[55]

This favorable assessment of Feininger's position among his Berlin colleagues seems to be somewhat the result of preconceived notions. Since Feininger was born a "Yankee"—whatever that might mean to the German reading public—some of the American flavor of his humor was explained as "Yankee snobbery," of which Feininger was free at all times. Hermann's comment that in spite of these native traces Feininger had developed a "typical Berlin humor, which is nevertheless his own" is especially meaningless since there is little of typical Berlin humor in his cartoons, although he occasionally used Berlin dialect in the captions.

Feininger's appearance at that time—tall, lean, dressed in loosely fitting sport clothes—and the fact that he was born in America—may have led his German critics to find typically American qualities in his art. Thirty years later Ludwig Thormaehlen[56] discovered a "boyish" quality in his mature work because the middle-aged American appeared still extremely youthful to the German.

A study of the cartoons Feininger drew for the Berlin humor magazines in the decade from 1894 to 1904 reveals that he was somewhat influenced by the style of the leading caricaturists for the Munich periodicals *Simplicissimus* and *Jugend*—such men as Thomas Theodore Heine, Bruno Paul, Ernst Heilemann, and Rudolf Wilke. Wilke[57] and Paul[58] are mentioned in a letter to Kortheuer written February 23, 1898:

> Shall send today: the title page to the *Jugend* (Carnival number). . . . It is made by Rudolf Wilke, whose name you must note as one of the most talented caricaturists in Germany. He is very young. As technician he is almost without equal. Bruno Paul is also fine, and in his way equals Wilke. He is more a satirist, whereas Wilke is the more refined and artistically superior of the two.

Feininger was never guilty of directly copying the manner of these artists, but he drew noticeable inspiration from the new style which developed toward the end of the century. He acknowledged this debt in an earlier letter to Kortheuer (January 30, 1898).

> I admire much that is in the modern direction but am distinctly individual in my work, so that I am coming in demand as modern and yet as original. Others copy me much, tho I could never pretend to be able to create followers in the strict sense. I crave after serious work and that is what I mean to turn to, when I can properly study.

There *was* a relationship between Feininger and what he called the modern direction—such movements as *Jugendstil,* or *Art Nouveau*—in spite of Hans Hess's disclaimer.[59] But Hess was certainly

30. Cover illustration for *Narrenschiff*. 1898.

31. *"Off with the Pigtail"* (*"Zopf ab"*).
Book jacket illustration. Circa 1900.

DER BLUTREGEN

ist aus Afrika bis nach England
geweht worden und wird dort
zum Landregen.

32. *Blood Rain* (*Der Blutregen*). Color cartoon for *Ulk*. 1901.

correct when he wrote that Feininger kept away from the *fin de siècle* mood and never smothered the clarity of his design with excessive undulant ornamentation. Still, when Feininger drew cartoons involving turn-of-the-century theater, art exhibits, or fashions, he quite naturally gave them the flavor of the period as his colleagues on *Jugend* and *Simplicissimus* did in their cartoons. Especially sucessful is his cartoon in *Ulk* (1896) entitled *Art Exhibit* (*Kunst Ausstellung*) in which modernity and antiquity are ludicrously fused by dressing archaic Grecian statuary in *Jugendstil* fashions.

In another *Ulk* cartoon (1896) entitled *At German Literature's Fountain of Youth* (*Am Jungbrunnen Deutscher Poesie*) Feininger contrasts the realistic side of Gerhart Hauptmann, Max Fulda, and Hermann Sudermann with their idealistic, romantic side. The gable of the House of Romantic Fantasy (Märchendichtung) in the drawing is transformed into the head of the maiden "Rautendelein" from Hauptmann's play *The Sunken Bell*, and framed by the curly waves of her long blonde hair. The aforementioned authors, having rejuvenated themselves at the Fountain of Youth within the house, file out into the open while the defeated spirit of Ibsen stands alone on one side, taking on the appearance of one of Feininger's ghosts. The drawing is decidedly in the *Art Nouveau* manner.

Feininger's relationship to the *Simplicissimus* and *Jugend* draftsmen was noticeable also in the field of society cartoons; aspects of the *Jugendstil* style are blended with personal vision of that world, in which imagination mingles with his characteristic observation of mechanisms.

George Hermann acutely observed:

He shows an incisive understanding for everything which is connected with modern machines, with the technique of transportation by ship. Like Rudyard Kipling he invests with life old thick-necked locomotives, which creep through the night with glowing eyes, strangely shaped air-ships, tropical boats with billowing sails and with an intricate, old-fashioned rigging. Modern white and gray battleships turn into iron monsters, spitting fire. But he is at his best in his caricatures of bicyclists. He is the psychologist of the wheel and of the sportsman . . . of all those who move by way of machines. He has evaluated this factor of our modern culture from the standpoint of the caricaturist.[60]

Feininger—himself an avid bicycle-rider—did some of his most humorous and penetrating cartoons about cycling. They were featured in *Sporthumor* and in the quite sophisticated and artistically progressive *Narrenschiff*. The cartoon *In the Bicycle Riders' Clinic* (*In der Radfahr-Klinik*, fig. 34) has a detailed, linear style; its earnest scientific realism creates the humorous effect. Another, *Balance*,[61] showing bicycle racers, contains the germ of Feininger's cubist painting of 1912 discussed on page 128. In *Easter Tour* of the *"Greased Chain" Bicycle Club* (*Ostertour des Radler-Klub "Geschmierte Kette,"* fig. 35) the emphasis is on the listless features of the fatigued Sunday bikers.

Feininger's multi-colored 1898 cover for *Narrenschiff* (see fig. 30) is artistically the best of the series. Composition, color contrast (blue-gray with brown), and the contrast between the two cycling types convey the humor. Elimination of detail and a decorative flatness in the Japanese manner are more evident here than in any of the other early works.

Another cycling cartoon, *Rained Out* (*Eingeregnet*),[62] which pictures five professional riders forced to spend the day in a dismal country inn, has some typical Feininger distortions. The elongated figures with small heads and enormous feet may well be caricatures of himself; Feininger later pictured himself as extremely tall and wearing grotesquely big shoes in his first drawing for "The Kin-der-Kids." Another *Narrenrad* drawing, *Grandpa at the Wheel* (*Grosspapa auf dem Rad*, fig. 33),[62] also displays this later cartoon style.

Feininger was always enthusiastic about devices that devoured space and time, yet there was a certain ambivalence in his attitude toward these manifestations of progress. In the cartoons he was to do for *Le Témoin*, his figures whirl like dry leaves over the city's

33. *Grandpa at the Wheel* (*Grosspapa auf dem Rad*). Pen cartoon for *Narrenrad*. Circa 1898.

In der Radfahr-Klinik.

Eine Operation.

Sanitäts-Wache.

ärztliche Untersuchung

No 713.
Hochgradiger
Fußtritt.

Kranken-
Pflegerin

die Luft-Kur.

34. *In the Bicycle Clinic* (*In der Radfahr-Klinik*). Pen cartoon for *Ulk*. 1897.

Ostertour des Radler-Klub „Geschmierte Kette".

Leonel Feininger.

„Sehen Sie, Kollege, bei 150 Kilometer, da fängt doch eigentlich erst das Vergnügen an."

35. *Easter Tour of the "Greased Chain" Bicycle Club* (*Ostertour des Radler-Klub "Geschmierte Kette"*).
Color cartoon for *Narrenschiff*. Circa 1898.

pavements. One of these cartoons, entitled *Exactitude* (1907),[64] has the sub-caption: "Where are we going?" "I don't know." "Then let's hurry." ("Où allons-nous? Je n'en sais rien. Alors pressons.") The editor of *Le Témoin* at that time, Paul Iribe, wrote the dialog, but the words expressed perfectly Feininger's antipathy to the age of speed. In 1949, after his return to America, he executed a watercolor of this drawing and called it *Hurrying-Where?*—a condensed version of the original caption.

Feininger longed for the charm of a vanished pre-industrial age. The generation that grew up around 1900 knew a world blackened by smoke from factory chimneys and fast-moving trains. Often it was the artists who felt most keenly the loss of a simpler, "purer" life. If they had the gifts of irony and imagination, they wrapped this nostalgia in the cloak of the grotesque and adorned it with the trappings of the late eighteenth and early nineteenth century. Georg Hermann spoke of this side of Feininger's humor as "quaint ideas" and "fairy-tale fantasy of compelling humor." As an example he reproduced a watercolor, *New Year's Eve's Ghost*, from the *Narrenschiff* of 1897.[65] Without a caption, it tells its story through two ghostly characters in old-fashioned clothes, one grotesquely thin, the other chubby. They are accompanied by a black cat, the traditional symbol of witchcraft. In Germany the black cat also symbolizes a *Katzenjammer*, or hangover. Feininger's flight into fancies of the past was certainly a reaction against the mechanical civilization so mistrusted by his elders—his father must often have reminisced about an unspoiled and meaningful culture that he knew in his youth. When Feininger stayed in rural New England as a child, he too experienced the solitude and leisurely pace of a countryside largely unchanged by the industrial revolution, and later he was captivated by the legacy of medieval Belgium.

The German artistic movement known as the Biedermeier Revival[66] crystallized these early experiences for Feininger.

The Biedermeier Revival became strong in the artistic centers, first in Munich and shortly thereafter in Berlin. The first issues of the progressive satirical magazines *Jugend* and *Simplicissimus* (both founded in Munich during 1896) pictured the costumes and the sentiments of "Grandfather Time" in the contributions of such artists as H. Caspari, Julius Diez, and, especially, Thomas Theodore Heine.[67] There, Biedermeier was amalgamated with the linearfloral patterns of *Jugendstil*, or *Art Nouveau*, and with the decadent elegance of the most brilliant representative of the English Aesthetic Movement, Aubrey Beardsley. Feininger specifically mentions the magazine *Jugend* in a letter to Churchill of January 29, 1898: "[I sent you] one of the better numbers of the Muenchner "Jugend," [it] might be welcome to you as an Anregung [inspiration] in the stilistisch [stylistic] or decorative line." Georg Hermann noted that the Biedermeier style was "conspicuous among some modern draftsmen"[68] but did not name Feininger among them, possibly because Feininger did not fully develop this tendency until some time after Hermann's 1901 study on caricature was published. This style is evident in Feininger's cartoons, etchings, and early paintings between 1905 and 1911, and occasionally in his later works.

During his stay in Paris in 1908, he made a colored lithograph for *Sporthumor* called *In 1840*. It depicts an oddly mechanized Biedermeier Age. Riding in some kind of a steam-driven car are a gentleman who looks very much like Abraham Lincoln and a pretty lady wearing an enormous crinoline and a hat with a veil; they are admired by elegant pedestrians in the costumes of the same era.[69] Feininger's contributions to the serious Berlin magazine *Schwarz und Weiss* (*Black and White*) in 1911 are also set in the world of Biedermeier.

In his graphics and paintings between 1905 and 1911, Feininger often showed tall and long-legged or short and fat men dressed in an amusing mixture of Biedermeier frock coats and Anglo-American sport clothes in the current fashion—made of boldly checked or striped material and worn with picturesque scarves. They smoke pipes or look through telescopes at sailing ships, as Feininger himself loved to do. Others blow trumpets or read large newspapers. Some are sinister gossips or scandalmongers. Many wear stovepipe hats, usually black and exaggeratedly high and narrow. To Feininger this comic yet sinister headgear was the true symbol of Biedermeier.

The symbolism of the Biedermeier stovepipe hat is still quite apparent in his later pictures, for instance in *Old American Locomotive,* which he worked on at intervals from 1914 to 1924.[70] To the right of the old locomotive is a group of top-hatted men standing together like participants in a funeral. In front of the vehicle, which has apparently served out its days or is stopping for an unlimited time, the ghost-like engineer appears in contrasting light color. The two motifs of the locomotive and the men in stovepipe hats are present in Feininger's work until the last years; these sinister men sometimes ride in the rickety toy trains over high viaducts which were recollections of Feininger's boyhood daydreams.

Feininger was not the only artist of his time to use the Biedermeier top hat as a symbol. The top hat and other period pieces like the Empire chest play similar symbolic roles of relics from the past in early short stories by Thomas Mann, such as "Tobias Mindernickel" (1897) and "The Way to the Churchyard" (*Simplicissimus,* Munich, 1901).[71]

Thomas Mann had been a "lector" or reader in the offices of *Simplicissimus* in Munich during the last years before the turn of the century. Mann, like Feininger, was also a bicycle enthusiast;[72] both were not only avid cyclists, but used the bicycle as a symbol of the modern life which had outdistanced and sometimes overrun the old times and their quaint, sad representatives. The Feininger-Mann parallel is especially evident in "The Way to the Churchyard," in which Lobgott Piepsam, a relic of the old times, "clad in black and wearing a rough curved top hat," assaults a young cyclist who symbolises modern life.

The Russian painter Wassily Kandinsky, then living in Munich, also introduced elaborate Biedermeier costumes into his oil of 1909, *Group in Crinolines*[73] (S. R. Guggenheim Museum, New York).

The bright, unreal colors and the distortions of the figures are curiously reminiscent of Feininger's work of only a few years earlier, especially his oil *Arceuil I,* of 1907 (Oeuvre Catalog No. 24). The irony and nostalgia which Mann and Kandinsky shared with Feininger and which found symbolic expression in a Biedermeier period style were the products of a cultural pessimism. "Ironic arabesques of a melancholy Anglo-Saxon Spitzweg"—so the critic Willy Wolfradt[74] referred to Feininger's Biedermeier penchant of these years.

The Biedermeier wave reached its height in 1906 with the Exhibition of German Art of the Period from 1775–1875 in the Royal National Gallery in Berlin.[75] This large assembly of forgotten treasures included paintings by Spitzweg and the romantic landscapist Caspar David Friedrich. Friedrich's romanticism in pictures of the Baltic Sea and the island of Rügen (both so dear to Feininger from his repeated stays there), of magnificently rigged sailing ships, of crow-gabled old towns and Gothic ruins, have been mentioned[76] as being parallel to works by Feininger.

More important than the choice of identical subject matter were the often eerie color schemes, the mysticism of light, the use of figures and even silhouettes before the majestic background of sea and sky, and the profoundly meditative mood quality of these pictures. Yet it is certain that this similarity is based on a related attitude toward nature and man's position in nature rather than on an actual study of Friedrich's paintings by Feininger, for he did not come to know Friedrich's work until 1926,[77] when he had already reached maturity as an artist. It is possible Feininger never saw the centennial exhibit; that same summer he left Berlin for Paris, arriving there on July 24, 1906.

IV
FROM CARTOONING TO PAINTING

Paris and Berlin, 1907–1912

The great change in Feininger's life occurred during his second stay in Paris: he became a painter. During the years spent as a successful caricaturist he had gained clarity of the inner workings, the deepest motivations of the cartoon-artist. His best definition of such an artist is found in a letter to Frau Julia:

A human being which feels everything stronger and beyond the prescribed norm. That pertains especially to all things of 'Beauty.' . . . No wonder that we of the caricaturist tribe, we caricaturists of true sentiment, all turn into melancholics.[1]

Dissatisfied with that prospect and fretting under the limitations and frustrations of his job, he had periodically voiced the need for greater scope in his art: "I crave serious work and that is what I mean to turn to, when I can properly study. (To Kortheuer, January 30, 1898)

I don't love these things, caricatures and whatnot, but they are simply the outcome of artistic Ohnmacht [frustration] to realize the beautiful. The quietly, reposefully beautiful I can never hope to reach, for I am too extravagant in feeling, but I am stirring towards something better, nevertheless, than this output of distortion. (To Churchill, January 14, 1899)

If I had only been left to have my choice of a calling I should have turned to some engineering or constructive calling for dead-sure. Well, here I sit, a success in a way, but just for that reason unable to leave the scene of my success, since I should have to begin all over again. So it is, that I am cut off from my youth's friends, from my country and all it has of sights and memories for me.

I've been over 16 years here and am 32 years old, it will soon be the half of my life. And consider me after all these years still a typical American, oozing from every pore, so that on the street I continually am pointed out by passers-by as "ein echter Amerikaner." . . . Well, I suppose, I'll get over [there] some day, but when, the Gods only know! (To Kortheuer, November 28, 1903)

Three years later he made the break. With his wife Julia, from then on his companion in all his artistic endeavors, Feininger began a new life by leaving Berlin and setting up a household in Paris. He would devote himself almost entirely to painting; but in the beginning it was still necessary to produce the cartoons which brought in money, such as the two strips he provided each week for the *Chicago Sunday Tribune.*

Feininger did his finest work as a cartoonist with the drawings he made in Paris shortly before he gave up cartooning permanently. He no doubt felt that such work was a deadening artistic compromise made merely for the sake of money. Yet in these cartoons, and in the ones for *Le Témoin,* there are ideas which gained fuller expression in his early paintings. He had often written to Churchill and Kortheuer of "fantasie" or "pure humor"; now the wit of his cartoons evolved into a kind of metaphysical humor which was to suffuse his works as a painter.

Shortly after arriving in Paris in the summer of 1906, Feininger met the painter Oskar Moll and his wife Margarete, herself a fine sculptress and painter.

They were soon among the first pupils in the school conducted by Matisse. At that time they were both groping for something beyond German impressionism, a style in which Oskar Moll had already achieved considerable success. In an interview with Peter Selz, Feininger recalled that he tried painting outdoors "in the manner of Monet and Liebermann under the guidance of Moll." The medium as well as the technique was new to him; he had never painted in oils before.

In a letter to the author in 1958, Margarete Moll recalled the events of more than fifty years before:

I met in Berlin in the year 1906 Feininger's charming mother, who taught voice. She persuaded me to become her pupil. . . . When in the fall of 1907 we went to Paris, we were asked to bring to Feininger greetings from his mother. We looked him up shortly after our arrival. He was a delightful man. Soon he joined Oskar on painting-trips to St. Cloud and the Luxembourg gardens. He had started painting in the summer but did not yet sufficiently master a technique new to him. We met him once on a Sunday morning, Purrmann had joined us. Oskar encouraged him after he had observed him at work, but Purrmann gave him a tongue-lashing, called it weak, girlish stuff. . . . Even today I still feel keenly the awkwardness of this situation. But maybe it helped Feininger in finding his own way. They introduced us to the circle of the Café du Dôme: Levy, Grossmann, Pascin. We saw then a great deal of the Feiningers and were always well received.

Mrs. Moll also tells of these first months in Paris in a letter to Alfred Barr, Jr.[3]

We had decided in the fall of 1907 to spend the winter in Paris, and since I knew Feininger's mother well, we visited Feininger on one of our first days of our stay in Paris. Through him we met Purrmann, Grossmann, Levy. At the end of the first week we came to know Matisse.

Mrs. Moll's letters indicate that Feininger was in contact with a certain group of German artists (except for Jules Pascin, who was born in Bulgaria) who throughout their long stay in Paris were most influential in bringing to Germany the art of the post-impressionists—Cézanne, Gauguin, Van Gogh and the Fauvists, especially Matisse. Feininger was not eager to embrace the new artistic creed, but he went to many of the exhibits at the Salon d'Automne, the galleries of the progressive art dealers, and to the studios of the artists themselves like Matisse, whose studio was open to all every Thursday afternoon.[4]

In 1912 Feininger wrote a sketch in elegant French of his development as an artist that was published in *Les Tendances nouvelles*. He stated that the great show at the Bernheim Jeune Galleries in 1907 (with works by Cézanne and Van Gogh) was a revelation to him.[5] Feininger must also have heard heated discussions about the work of the avant-garde in the Café du Dôme: "Let us talk again about Cézanne" was the refrain of a witty poem by Levy that originated at the Dôme.[6]

Impressionism was out of fashion. Even such artists as Moll and Purrmann, who up to then had worked in the style, now rejected it. Oskar Moll (1875–1947) had been a pupil of Corinth and Leistikow in Berlin from 1897 on. In the fall of 1907, when he painted outdoors with Feininger, Moll had not yet entered the Matisse school, although he had met Matisse and seen his paintings. The earliest work by Moll that shows Matisse's influence is *Girl at the Window*, painted a few months after he became a pupil in 1908. So it is doubtful that Moll was responsible for introducing a Fauvist note in Feininger's paintings of 1907, as Selz seems to suggest.[7]

Still lifes, landscapes, and views of Paris are the earliest of Feininger's oils mentioned in the Oeuvre Catalog compiled by Mrs. Julia Feininger. Among them are two still lifes (dated April 21 and 22), *Villa on the Seine I* and *II*, and *Arcueil I*, all from 1907. The style of some of these early paintings—the still lifes, for example—is German impressionist. Feininger's manner in others is close to the treatment in his *Témoin* cartoons; *Arcueil* shows Biedermeier characters in front of a high viaduct. All are painted in a dark, rough-textured impasto, resembling Monet less than the German forerunners of expressionism, such as Lovis Corinth.

There is, however, a strong flavor of Fauvism in the figural compositions of 1908 and 1909, especially in the large oil *The Manhole I* (1909, collection of Mrs. Julia Feininger; originally called *Child Murderess* [Kindsmörderin]).[8] The rail alongside the river is a brilliant Chinese red, the cobblestones are purplish-pink, the woman suspected of murdering her child has green skin and blue hair. This painting blends Feininger's last and most original cartoon style with Fauvism as it was practiced by the circle of the Café du Dôme.

The Dôme, now gone, reached its height in the twenties. The

Hamburg painter Friedrich Ahlers-Hestermann, himself a member of the Circle, gives this description of it in the old days:

> It was exactly as dingy as every other café of the same class. The pompous name derived from a small dome that crowned the sharp corner of the Boulevard Montparnasse and the rue Delambre, a modest and by no means conspicuous "fantasy" of the humdrum builder. . . . The greenish gaslight in the evening was neither conducive to conviviality nor did it improve the air. Here, at marble-topped tables, the German artists sat—only the devil knows why! . . .
>
> People have compared the 'Dôme' to a dingy waiting room in a depot. That fits not only the interior but also the people sitting there, alone and in groups. They all gave the impression they were waiting for something—for friends, for money, for that uncertain event which had brought them there, a possibility dreamt about but never to be realized.[9]

The small and inconspicuous café[10] had been discovered by Purrmann soon after he arrived in Paris in 1906, a young artist of twenty-six. He had studied at the Munich Academy but had come under the influence of the famous Berlin impressionist Max Liebermann. Purrmann went to Paris to improve his impressionist technique and to see the great Manet show of 1906. With his friend and countryman Leo Weisgerber, a promising young German artist who was killed in World War I, Purrmann made the Dôme an informal meeting-place for German artists in Paris. The circle included the painters Friedrich Ahlers-Hestermann and Rudolf Levy, the graphic artists Rudolf Grossmann and Jules Pascin, the sculptors Ernesto de Fiori and Wilhelm Lehmbruck, and the writers Wilhelm Uhde and Franz Hessel.

Some years later Ahlers-Hestermann and Levy became pupils of Matisse, but Purrman played the outstanding role in the organization of the Matisse school in 1908. Gertrude Stein, though not fond of Purrmann, called him "the bulwark of the Matisse school.[11] Rudolf Levy settled in Paris in 1903, before any of the other German artists. He became a pupil of Matisse in 1909. When

Feininger met him, Levy was an enthusiastic champion of Cézanne, whose memorial exhibit in the Salon d'Automne in 1907 had spread the fame of the master of Aix. Gauguin's art was shown in the Salon in 1906, the year of Matisse's most influential Fauvist painting, *Joie de Vivre*. Picasso, though he had already painted his first large cubist painting *Demoiselles d'Avignon* in 1907, was less known to the circle at the Dôme. Certainly Feininger knew nothing of him in 1907, when the term "cubism" was not yet in wide circulation.

Both Grossmann and Pascin had tried their hands at painting, but at that time they supported themselves chiefly with witty drawings and watercolors of Parisian low-life that bordered on caricature.

Feininger's closest friend among these artists was Jules Pascin (1885–1930),[12] who had also gained a considerable reputation as a contributor to satirical periodicals, chiefly *Simplicissimus*. After informal study in Vienna and Munich, he had come to Paris on Christmas Eve, 1905, received at the train by a delegation from the Dôme. Feininger met him at the Dôme a year later, and again in 1911, before this restless bohemian set out on the wanderings around the globe that brought him to New York in 1914. Pascin's graphic style, similar to *Art Nouveau,* had been formed through contact with the Vienna Secession. In his fine, often nervously scribbled yet flowing line, Pascin then was artistically most akin to Feininger. A pen drawing by Pascin published in *Simplicissimus* with the ironic title *People of Sentiment*[13] resembles Feininger's work around 1906–7 not only in the sensitive line but also in the odd, old-fashioned clothes worn by one of the men.

Pascin appears in two drawings which Feininger did in 1908: *Pascin with the Coffee Cup,*[14] and *Stammtafel* [reserved table] *im Café du Dôme.*[15] These drawings and the many quick pencil sketches which Feininger made in Paris show him to be a master of line and characterization. This mastery is particularly apparent in his portrait of a fellow student at the Atelier Colarossi (January 23, 1907)[16] where Feininger occasionally went to draw nudes.

In this portrait we again find the contrast between a small head and enormous feet that was the trademark of Feininger as a caricaturist.

Feininger continued to exaggerate height, shape, and dress when he pictured women of the advanced Paris art circles, as in *Women at the Exhibition,* a drawing in pen and watercolor of 1908.[17] Since the title was in German, this caricature was no doubt destined for a Berlin magazine; the style has the sharp bite of the drawings in *Ulk.*

Feininger encountered an atmosphere of artistic freedom and willingness to experiment at *Le Témoin,* the sophisticated French journal whose name meant *Witness,* i.e., to the foibles of society. The ideas and style of his drawings were left entirely up to him, although the editor might occasionally supply a caption. Feininger had not known such freedom before.

The co-founder of *Le Témoin* was the painter Wilhelm Howard,[18] one of the lesser members of the Dôme circle. The rather comical and corpulent Howard claimed descent from Catherine Howard and posed as pretender to the English Crown, in spite of the fact that he came from Leipzig. As an artist he was a figure of minor significance, but he was no doubt the person who introduced Feininger to Paul Iribe, the editor of *Le Témoin* at that time.

Iribe was a true artist, and one of the first of Feininger's employers to sense and encourage his unique genius. None of the Feininger drawings which appeared during Iribe's brief tenure as editor of *Le Témoin* (from Oct. 1906 to April 1907) are cartoons or caricatures in the usual sense; only a sophisticated and perceptive viewer could fully appreciate their subtle humor. It was Iribe who so brilliantly interpreted the frenzied movement of the two figures in the 1907 drawing *Exactitude* with the caption quoted previously (on p. 93). Two other cartoons that Iribe published without descriptive captions, commentary, or dialog in 1907 were *L'Exode*[19] and *L'Impatiente (La Belle).*[20] The humor in these drawings is visual, aided only by the brief titles. The subject of *L'Exode* is the expulsion of the Jesuits from Paris. It reveals Feininger's close study of "Jesuit physiognomy" during his stay at the college in Liège. *L'Impatiente* represents with delicacy and poignancy a beauty of the streets, dressed with the fashionable yet provocative elegance of her profession: high-heeled button shoes, a flaring skirt, and a generous display of undergarments. Very tall and thin, she stands against a sinister background of high, old Parisian houses with their characteristic chimneys. The "Impatient Beauty" possessed certain poetic possibilities as *femme fatale* which Feininger embodied in one of his masterpieces of fifteen years later, *Lady in Mauve* (*La Dame en Mauve*).[21]

In the cartoons of 1906 and 1907 which later provided material for paintings, one can see clearly the evolution of Feininger's art, his transformation into a painter. These products of his most mature cartoon style were far above the level of usual works of the kind. Perhaps they show as well that an extraordinary cartoon could very well provide the germ for a good modern painting. Eberhard Ruhmer expresses the same idea in his book on Feininger:

The aspect of the caricaturist has much in common with that of the modern anticlassical artist. It can be assumed that caricature is one of the historical prerequisites of modern art. Who could fail to see caricature in the expressive deformation of a Schmidt-Rottluff, a Nolde or Kokoschka?[22]

Two other 1907 cartoons exemplify this transition stage in Feininger's development: *The Prudent Schemer* (*Le Prévoyant Fraudeur*, fig. 36) and *Moloch à Paris* (fig. 37); both originally appeared in *Le Témoin* in most attractive color. In *The Prudent Schemer* the wings of the windmill and the angle of the building anticipate similar effects in such somber and majestic paintings as *The Mill* of 1918.[23] The exaggerated contrast (here of the giant miller to his gnomelike, imbecilic son, the future chemist) is a device Feininger used to gain not only humorous results in these cartoons but also powerful effects in his later prints and paintings. *Moloch à Paris* creates ambiguities through purely visual means. The grouchy, ferociously bearded relic of the past with his funny hat of uncertain vintage and old-fashioned cape seems to disapprove of sinful Paris, at least as long as one takes

37. *Moloch à Paris*. Color cartoon for *Le Témoin*. 1906.

36. **The Prudent Schemer (*Le Prevoyant Fraudeur*).**
Color cartoon for *Le Témoin*. 1907.

the title literally. Yet his eyes belie the text and reveal him as a secret worshiper of that Moloch who is fed with human flesh. The hidden meaning and its consequent humor are conveyed by a few lines and glances, a minimum of costume, but chiefly by contrasts in position, direction, and texture.

Feininger was a critic of the contemporary scene in *Le Témoin.* His topics were social rather than political. His setting was a Paris of reality mixed with fantasy—dim and shadowy narrow streets bordered by old houses with their forest of high chimneys and surmounted by Gothic towers like the Tour St. Jacques. *L'Impatiente,* and a strange, very tall man with a broad-brimmed black felt hat who smokes an English "shack" pipe as he slouches down the night streets,[24] are typical of the figures who haunt the rather sinister and menacing environment. Feininger made a drawing of the latter figure for *Le Témoin* in 1907; later that year he translated it into a painting. To both he gave the cryptic title *The White Man.* The giant ghost seems an emanation of Feininger's other, shadowy self.

In these drawings the houses are composed of diagonals and the figures are slanted, often at a sharp angle. For both figures and architecture Feininger used broadly decorative, poster-like effects. There is an inexhaustible variety of textural pattern in these drawings. They must have particularly appealed to Paul Iribe, one of the champions of Japonism in Paris.

There are similarities between Feininger's career and that of his much younger contemporary, the Spaniard Juan Gris, who later played such an important role in the cubist movement. Gris worked for *Le Témoin* at the same time as Feininger, both having been brought in by the publication's editor, Iribe. Like Feininger, Gris drew cartoons for the progressive Parisian magazines which revealed his artistic stature and prepared him for his later work as a painter. Born in Madrid in 1887, Gris had come to Paris when he was nineteen and joined his compatriot Picasso in the "Bâteau Lavoir," the slum building whose studios sheltered so many great artists. The amazingly precocious Gris, like Feininger, brought nothing to Paris but his skill as a caricaturist. It brought him immediate work for *Le Témoin, L'Assiette au Beurre,* and some of the less progressive magazines such as *Le Charivari* and *Le Cri de Paris.*

The similarities between Feininger and Gris extend to their work, both in style and subject. Early in his career Gris felt the influence of *Art Nouveau* and worked in this style in Spain. But his drawings for the Paris magazines more strongly show the impact of Japonism, which blended easily with the undular ornamentation of *Art Nouveau.* James Thrall Soby speaks of Juan Gris's "refinement of calculation and highly original color sense."[25] The same could be said about Feininger's cartoons of that time. Gris's crowded street scenes resemble Feininger's in their angularity and frequent emphasis on decorative pattern. *The Automobilist*[26] whose hands resemble claws in a grim cartoon of 1910 shows Gris, like Feininger, worshipping as well as attacking the new god of speed. There are many similarities between the work of the two artists at this time, although no record of a direct contact between the two men has so far been discovered.

However, another famous figure in Parisian art circles, Julius Meier-Graefe,[27] was most probably known to Feininger. Although this brilliant writer on modern art did not resume his permanent residence in Paris until 1910, he visited the Dôme circle occasionally on one of his numerous Paris visits. Around the turn of the century he had played an important part in introducing the work of German designers and book-artists to the fashionable galleries of Paris. He had also been acquainted with Paul Iribe, whose interests in Japonism he shared. Generally speaking, he was the most efficient liaison-officer between the art and artists of Germany and France. It is due chiefly to his efforts that French Impressionism became so well known in Germany and the rest of Europe. In 1896 he had assisted S. Bing in the shop in the Rue de Provence which gave its name to the movement—*Art Nouveau.* In 1897–8 he founded *L'Art Décoratif,* the French edition of *Dekorative Kunst,* the Munich magazine he had also begun. In 1899 he opened his own gallery of decorative art, the *Maison Moderne*. It did much to bring German *Jugendstil* into the art of Paris.

Feininger was never an enthusiastic follower of *Jugendstil*, but he weakened somewhat when he was commissioned by the Berlin publisher Hans Bondy to illustrate a book of Scandinavian fairy tales for children in the *Jugendstil* manner then in vogue. Bondy was a relative of the painter Walter Bondy, who for ten years (1903–13) was a member of the Dôme circle. The publisher would visit the Dôme on his frequent visits to Paris; it was there that he met Feininger. The very title of the book, *Norwegische Volksmärchen für die Jugend bearbeitet* (*Norwegian Fairy Tales Edited for Young Readers*),[28] must have appealed to Feininger; earlier in his career he had stressed "pure fantasy," ghosts and goblins and nonsense stories in his illustrations for American boys' magazines. That this collection was full of odd and fantastic stories may have been what brought publisher and artist together. Feininger had up to this time illustrated only one book for German publishing houses: Max Dreyer's *Das Tal des Lebens* (*The Valley of Life*), which appeared in Leipzig in 1904 (*Stuttgart und Deutsche Verlagsanstalt*).[29]

It seems on the surface an odd situation: a German publisher meets an American cartoonist in Paris and entrusts him with the illustration of some old Scandinavian fairy tales. Nevertheless, Feininger did a beautiful job of blending the apparently disparate and incongruous elements. He must have done careful reasearch in libraries and museums for ornamental Viking motifs, yet they are so amalgamated in the overall design that they never seem merely pedantic or antiquarian.

Especially in England, but also in Germany and Austria, *Art Nouveau* flourished as a style for book design and illustration. Feininger adapted its refined and often precious ornamental forms to his own "pure fantasy and nonsense" manner, ennobling them with his particular brand of philosophical and whimsical humor. Feininger made sixteen full-size plates, half of them in color, as well as drawings for the title page and initials. These illustrations are another important step in his evolution from cartoonist to fantasist.

He lavished his love and expert knowledge on the depiction of many highly decorative Viking ships. His dragons and dragon-heads are fantastic and original. The ornamental waves recall Hokusai's famous color prints. Figures are either exceptionally elongated or dwarfish. The textures of tree trunks are exciting. There is a wealth of abstract ornament. In the black-and-white drawing for the story *Die drei Muhmen* (*The Three Aunts*) (fig. 38) we see the ornamental decorativeness, whimsical humor, mastery of the medieval setting, and sheer fantasy which characterize Feininger's illustrations for the *Norwegische Volksmärchen*. The three aunts startle the poor girl who is now queen. One has an especially long nose, another has an enormous backside, and the third has eyes as big as saucers. Most admirable—and prophetic of the painter—are the daring color combinations used in the eight colored plates.

Viaducts always fascinated Feininger; the one in Meudon was a favorite during his stay in Paris. In his illustration for another of the stories, *Die Drei Böcke Brauswind* (*The Three Storm Goats*), he puts a goat on one of his typical high viaducts.

Feininger's style as a fantasist was as much his personal creation as it was a product of the era. Yet his illustrations for the *Norwegische Volksmärchen* are somewhat similar in style to the enchanting pictures which the Viennese publishing house of Martin Gerlach commissioned from outstanding artists for its *Jugend-bücherei* (*Library for the Young*). In the use of ornamental line, the booklets designed and illustrated by the very talented Hugo Steiner-Prag are especially close to Feininger's style. Steiner-Prag was an exponent of the Vienna Secession variety of *Jugendstil*; another artist then active in the movement was Oskar Kokoschka. In 1908, the year the *Norwegische Volksmärchen* was published, Kokoschka made an important contribution with his color lithographs for *Träumende Knaben* (*Dreaming Boys*), also a children's book. These lithographs also bear a certain period relationship to

38. *The Three Aunts* (*Die drei Muhmen*).
Illustration from *Norwegische Volksmärchen*. 1908.

Feininger's illustrations. But Feininger's graphic art totally lacked the characteristic *Art Nouveau* element of languishing decadence; possibly his inherent Americanism kept him from inclining toward it. (He was entertaining the American public with his comic strips at the time.)

During this period Feininger drew for publications in America, France, and Germany—a rare achievement. It would be difficult to find another draftsman who simultaneously served three cultures as variously and as well. But his artistic situation was paradoxical. In order to become a modern, unconventional painter he tried to suppress and even extinguish his penchant for cartooning and illustrating just when he had attained his greatest skill in these fields. Yet the distortions and other traditional liberties of the cartoonist served as his pathway to the avant-garde of French painting.

Just before leaving Berlin for his second stay in Paris, Feininger had rejected an opportunity to return to the United States as a cartoonist. James Keeley of the *Chicago Tribune* had come to Germany scouting for talent and had proposed that Feininger immediately accompany him back to the United States and join the *Tribune* staff. This created a serious dilemma for Feininger, who had decided to abandon cartooning, but it was finally agreed that he could mail his cartoons from Europe. Feininger worked almost daily for half a year on the drawings and text for two comic strips he sent to the *Chicago Tribune:* "The Kin-der-Kids" and "Wee Willie Winkie's World."

He sent his first contribution on March 5, 1906—an announcement of "The Kin-der-Kids" that was published on April 29. The strip, which ran as a regular feature twenty-four times from May 6 to November 18, was well under way by the time the Feiningers settled in Paris at 242 Boulevard Raspail on July 24. "Wee Willie Winkie's World" began on August 19, 1906, and ran twenty-eight times, until January 20, 1907. The names for the two cartoons were probably found with the aid of Keeley, though the ideas were entirely Feininger's. While "Wee Willie Winkie" derived from a character in a well-known English nursery rhyme, "The Kin-der-Kids," by the clipped rhythm and alliteration in their title, demonstrate their bilingual character and their origin in a German-American setting. It is even more than likely that the title and the strip were actually intended to be competitive with those of the "Katzenjammer Kids."

This strip was created by Rudolf Dirks in 1897, almost ten years before "The Kin-der-Kids," for William Randolph Hearst's *New York Journal.* While in Germany, Hearst had come across Wilhelm Busch's children's book, *Max and Moritz* (1859), and brought it to America. In his young staff artist, Rudolf Dirks, Hearst had found the man who could work up a strip based on these two formidable brats and troublemakers. Dirks maintained their Germanic identity by changing their names to "Hans and Fritz," and having them speak a kind of make-believe German dialect. However, the setting for their pranks and adventures is a tropical island, while that of Feininger's "Kin-der-Kids" is in the main Germanic, consisting of gothic church steeples, high, pitched roofs, half-timbered houses, and narrow, crooked streets paved with cobblestones. This quasi-medieval milieu contrasts most effectively with the strip's super-modern, typically American gadgetry, fantastic flying machines, and the family bathtub-boat, which on one occasion ventures across the Atlantic. In one of the figures —Japanski, the clockwork waterbaby—Feininger even anticipates the robot.

In these children's cartoons Feininger realized his youthful dream and brought his personal nonsense style to fruition. Although both comic strips ran for less than a year, a span of time too brief to make a lasting impression on the general public or on the historians and critics of the popular arts, they established one of the early precedents for unbridled whimsy, fantasy, and sophisticated style in the American cartoon. In "Wee Willie Winkie's World," the more philosophical of the two strips, a lonely child reveals to "Your uncle Feininger," the artist, "that the sun, trees, locomotives, puddles, ships, and clouds are living things with faces and feelings."[30] It is a gentle, lyrical world, certainly not beyond the understanding of sensitive children but probably even more appealing to adults.

"The Kin-der-Kids" was more definitely designed for children. It is highly dramatic—from jujitsu fights to adventures in boats, balloons, jails, and bird cages. The captions were racy and slangy. Utopian gadgetry and flying machines abounded. A cartoon strip published July 1, 1906 was entitled *Relief Expedition Slams into a Steeple with Results.* The balloon is the winner in this clash of the Old with the New as it carries off the Gothic steeple—a cat and a man still in it—over the storm-tossed sea. Another strip presents a most absurd and fantastic flying contraption. The caption reads: "She works like a charm. I've solved the problem of flying."[31] Both of these cartoons are reminiscent of the *Friedrich Strasse* and of the cartoons showing balloon expeditions that appeared in the Berlin humor magazines.

In his first cartoon for the strip, Feininger introduced the characters in "The Kin-der-Kids." The artist is identified as "Uncle Feininger" by a name tag pinned to his ear. As usual, he draws himself with very long legs that mock his height. His hands and feet are enormous, but he looks most friendly and avuncular as he peers over his glasses. His characters dangle from his fingertips like marionettes on strings. The names he found for them are typical of his humor, and coincide perfectly with their manner and appearance; they derive for the most part from his own German-American childhood. Their names are on labels attached to them: Aunty Jim-Jam, Cousin Gussy, Mr. Pillsbury, Sherlock Bones (the dachshund), Daniel Webster, Piemouth, Strenuous Teddy, Japansky the Clockwork Waterbaby, and Mysterious Pete. The editor advertised the new series with an announcement in large type: "Feininger the famous German artist exhibiting the characters he will create." Feininger was introduced to the American public as a German artist because of his long stay abroad, during which he had established his reputation as a cartoonist by his work for German periodicals.

39. First sketches for "The Kin-der-Kids."
Pen, crayon, watercolor. 1906
(date on sketch incorrect).

One of the original sketches for some of the characters in "The Kin-der-Kids" has remained in the possession of Mrs. Julia Feininger (fig. 39). In pen and ink, with color added in crayon, it has an inscription by Feininger: "First sketches for a comic serial: 'The Kin-der-Kids' drawn February 1907." It shows "Aunty Jim Jam," "Otto the Greenhorn," a "Policeman in a hurry," and two unnamed characters, one resembling Uncle Sam, the other a naughty-looking boy with Biedermeier-era tasseled cap and lacy pants. On the back of the paper are four more characters, two of them wearing stovepipe hats. On the sketch Mrs. Feininger has written, "Leo is mistaken, these first sketches were made in February 1906 before he went to Munich to meet Keeley from Chicago Tribune." This correction proves that the idea for "The Kin-der-Kids" was not suggested by Mr. Keeley but had occupied Feininger's imagination before they met.

The sketches show running figures whose liveliness and suggestion of speed are like those in today's animated cartoon characters, and static, puppet-like figurines, like those which dangle from the fingers of "Uncle Feininger" in the introductory cartoon.

We gain the fullest information concerning the appearance and activities of these characters in a multicolor sheet entitled "The Kin-der-Kids portrait gallery" (fig. 40). Daniel Webster with his distraught-looking dachshund Sherlock Bones is a precocious, constantly reading "quiz-kid": all forehead, as wizened as an old man, and gauntly undernourished. Pie-mouth, however, is constantly eating; Strenuous Teddy constantly training and lifting gigantic dumbbells and weights; Cousin Gussie and Aunty Jim-Jam are sinister New England characters wearing the costumes of the Pilgrim era. Similarly prim is the gloomy Mr. Pillsbury, the pill manufacturer, a gigantic figure with tiny hat and enormous shoes. His five daughters, identically dressed in their Sunday best, range like organ pipes from tall to short and from lean to fat. Mysterious Pete is half comic opera Robber-Chieftain, half "Leatherstocking." Little Japansky is a mechanical "clockwork waterbaby" who can exist under water when not wound up for action with his

The Kin-der-Kids portrait gallery

For the history of the Kin-der-Kids see inside pages

DANIEL WEBSTER.

PIE-MOUTH.

STRENUOUS TEDDY.

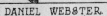

GUSSIE.   AUNT JIM-JAM.

THE PILLSBURY FAMILY.

UNCLE KIN-DER.

MYSTERIOUS PETE AND HIS HOUND.

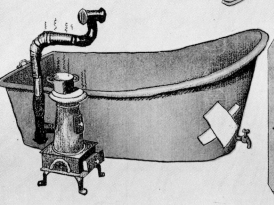

THE KIN-DER FAMILY BATH TUB

LITTLE JAPANSKY.

40. *"The Kin-der-Kids portrait gallery."*
Color cartoon series for the *Chicago Sunday Tribune*.
Entire series copyrighted 1906.

big key. Uncle Kin-der represents the German-American milieu, pig-faced, short, very corpulent, wearing big, heavy glasses and smoking an enormous German pipe with a porcelain bowl.

The Kin-der Family Bath Tub is a full-fledged "dramatis persona" in its own right and not merely a prop. Though battered, haphazardly patched with tape and badly in need of repair, it is comparable to the magic carpet in Eastern fairy tales. In the cartoon "The Kin-der-Kids abroad" it outraces the biggest Ocean liners in the triumphant departure of the Kids from New York harbor. The pursuers—Cousin Gussie and Aunty Jim-Jam—are left behind in their boat while the Statue of Liberty waves an encouraging farewell with a gargantuan handkerchief.

With the exception of the two cartoons which introduce "Uncle Feininger" and his characters, there is always breathless action. A typical Old World chimney sweep, "kindhearted Pat," who talks in a German-American version of Irish dialect, rescues Pie-mouth from a double dose of castor oil by hoisting him up through the chimney and escaping with him over the roofs of the pitch-gabled houses (fig. 41).

In another cartoon strip (fig. 42) the whole gang escapes from Aunty Jim-Jam and her castor oil through narrow streets, up and down staircases, finally jumping from a high dock into the family bath-tub which Japanski propels out of reach of the hotly pursuing adult. True to the anti-adult spirit of the strip, Aunty Jim-Jam is unable to stop in time when she reaches the end of the pier, and plunges into the water. "Geewhoop! she put down her Westinghouse brakes too late!"

"Wee Willie Winkie's World," Feininger's somewhat later and more mature cartoon, replaces physical action and speed by the animation of landscape and phenomena of nature as well as all so-called "dead objects." This metamorphosis takes place for the most part in a gradual way, but can also be quite sudden and startling—for instance in Feininger's handling of trees and clouds, ships and stones.

In a cartoon strip devoted to an outing of the little fellow

41. "The Kin-der-Kids." *Piemouth Is Rescued by Kind-Hearted Pat.*

42. "The Kin-der-Kids." *Narrow Escape from Aunty Jim-Jam.*

43. "Wee Willie Winkie's World." Color cartoon series for
the *Chicago Sunday Tribune*. Nov. 25, 1906.

(fig. 43), Willie is shown starting out on one of his lonely expeditions on what promises to be a fine day. "Great clouds with puffy windblown cheeks sailed through the sky." Everything seemed peaceful and ordinary enough, yet "one little leafless tree waved two stumpy little branch arms" and seemed to warn other trees nearby. The faces of the clouds are those of amused observers, while those of the trees suggest different stages of anxiety. Then the drama of nature gathers speed. "The farther on Willie went the stranger the trees acted."

In the second frame a group of slender birches tremble enigmatically. Large frightened eyes stare from their tops behind the tiny wanderer. This fantasy element is so perfectly fused with an exact rendering of reality that "trees with eyes" become the most logical and natural thing in the world. Feininger's loving observation and penetrating analysis of the structure and texture of trees make the situation entirely plausible. How many hundreds of trees must he have drawn to become so familiar with their character and organic structure! One might compare these trees with his pencil drawing of July 31, 1898, *The Road to Oranienburg* (Chausse nach Oranienburg) reproduced by Hess[32] with the group of trees described above. One observes in both the beginning of the process of stylization which leads to Feininger's "Prismism" in his later landscape paintings.

In the third frame of the strip the frightened trees seem to run up the hill, apparently chased by "long green caterpillars as big as dragons." Willie pauses to look again at the monsters—and discovers that they are only long rows of squat trees. And so everything ends peacefully; a cozy German village with a stout old church, the place "where grandpa lives," provides the happy ending—the stillness after the storm.

To the historian of art this particular cartoon series offers a number of leads to the origin of many motifs in Feininger's later pictures. In one of Willie's strolls along the seashore (fig. 44), sleepy old boats (one of them "a fat old uncle boat with glasses") are awakened by the incoming tide and swept into the sea. After

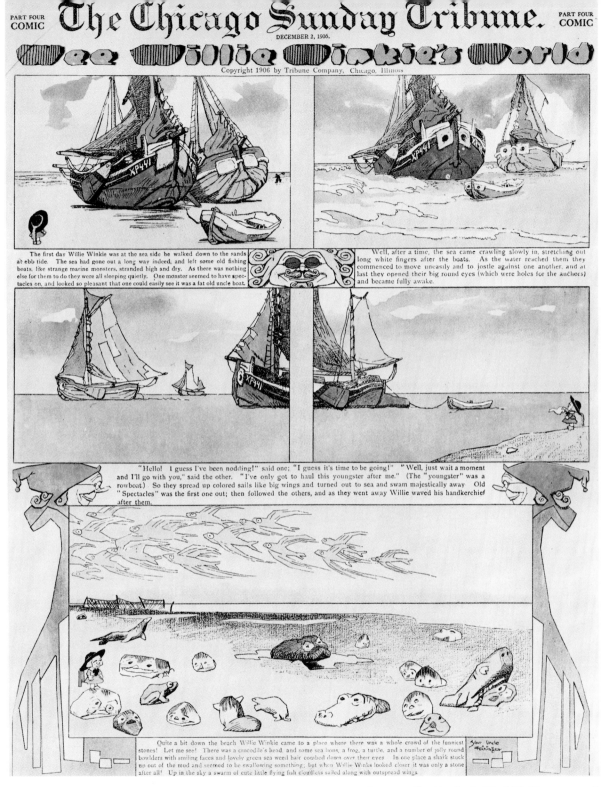

PART FOUR
COMIC

The Chicago Sunday Tribune.

PART FOUR
COMIC

DECEMBER 2, 1906.

Wee Willie Winkie's World

Copyright 1906 by Tribune Company, Chicago, Illinois

The first day Willie Winkie was at the sea side he walked down to the sands at ebb tide. The sea had gone out a long way indeed, and left some old fishing boats, like strange marine monsters, stranded high and dry. As there was nothing else for them to do they were all sleeping quietly. One monster seemed to have spectacles on, and looked so pleasant that one could easily see it was a fat old uncle boat.

Well, after a time, the sea came crawling slowly in, stretching out long white fingers after the boats. As the water reached them they commenced to move uneasily and to jostle against one another, and at last they opened their big round eyes (which were holes for the anchors) and became fully awake.

"Hello! I guess I've been nodding!" said one; "I guess it's time to be going!" "Well, just wait a moment and I'll go with you," said the other. "I've only got to haul this youngster after me." (The "youngster" was a rowboat.) So they spread up colored sails like big wings and turned out to sea and swam majestically away. Old "Spectacles" was the first one out; then followed the others, and as they went away Willie waved his handkerchief after them.

Quite a bit down the beach Willie Winkie came to a place where there was a whole crowd of the funniest stones! Let me see! There was a crocodile's head, and some sea lions, a frog, a turtle, and a number of jolly round bowlders with smiling faces and lovely green sea weed hair combed down over their eyes. In one place a shark stuck up out of the mud and seemed to be swallowing something; but when Willie Winks looked closer it was only a stone after all! Up in the sky a swarm of cute little flying fish cloudlets sailed along with outspread wings.

Your Uncle Feininger

44. "Wee Willie Winkie's World." Dec. 2, 1906.

they have sailed off, Willie, who would have liked so much to sail off with them, is left alone on the stones which lie scattered about on the beach in a profusion of sizes. Suddenly they too are transformed into "a number of jolly round boulders with smiling faces and lovely green seaweed hair combed down over their eyes. . . . Up in the sky a swarm of cute little flying fish cloudlets sailed along with outspread wings."

Here we have the early germ of two of Feininger's most wonderful seascapes: *Cloud after Storm* (Wolke nach dem Sturm) and *Bird Cloud* (Vogelwolke) of 1926. For the latter there exists an earlier (1924) pencil sketch after nature.[33]

In its bizarre and whimsical humor, which is so perfectly blended with the wisdom of "little people," animals and objects in nature, "Wee Willie Winkie" foreshadows the comic strip "Krazy Kat" begun by George Herriman in 1913, six years later. But the relationship between "Willie" and the "Kat" is only in spirit, in its mixture of fantasy and irony, not in the manner of drawing. In style, Feininger is unique, and in this respect his two "American" strips have no connection with the few earlier comic strips published in the United States up to 1907 and the swarm of funnies which came after that date. Feininger's achievement as cartoonist lies there like an erratic rock on the plains of the American comic strip.

As indicated, there may have been the intention to challenge the success of the "Katzenjammer Kids" of 1896 with "The Kinder-Kids," and there is certainly a thematic relationship which ultimately and in both instances goes back to the pranks of *Max and Moritz*, the common ancestors of all American cartoon Kids. Similarly, H. Arthur Klein remarks: "We may well call W. Busch the stepfather, if not the father, of an important group of comics in the United States."[34] Even the earliest of the "Kids" (1895), Richard Outcault's "The Yellow Kid" in his eternal long nightshirt, might be a poor cousin to that family. But the disgusting slum customs of the "Yellow Kid" (always sitting on a curbstone with a hangover) are a world apart from even the worst behaviour of that international gang, "The Kin-der-Kids."

In short, all other cartoon-Kids lack that peculiar blend of European sophistication and the raw puerilities of American manners found in the Kin-der crowd, a distinguishing quality which the European-American Feininger had bestowed on the brainchildren of his imagination and of his memories.

From the standpoint of general style, Feininger's two strips are related somewhat to European art movements of the *fin de siècle*. In its rich ornamental frames "Wee Willie Winkie" shows a connection with *Art Nouveau*, especially in the faces and figures of goblins appearing between the panels. They are definitely related to those Feininger drew for the *Norwegische Volksmärchen*. These illustrations were done in Paris at the same time as the cartoon strips.

Japonism, with its flat decorative patterns and omission of details, also exerted a certain influence on Feininger at that time (1906-7). Aline Louchheim relates that during an interview Feininger pointed to some of the Japanese prints which decorated his home and remarked: "In 1906 I wished to get some of that effect into my cartoons."[35] Yet there are traces of the Japanese print in some of his work for the Berlin magazines ten years earlier. In 1905, the year *before* he came to Paris, Feininger wrote:

Expressive simplicity can only be attained contrariwise inasmuch as one gradually learns to eliminate all superfluous details. Because one has learned to master them one may suppress them. That constitutes the highest degree of proficiency. One should always strive to achieve this.

The best information we now have about Feininger's artistic intentions during the years when his style as a painter was formed (1907-8) is contained in excerpts from letters which Mrs. Feininger made available for the catalog of an exhibit of his work in 1941. We read in a letter of 1906 that: "The slightest difference in relative proportions creates enormous differences with regard to the resulting monumentality of and intensity of the composition."[36]

How well this statement can be applied to the grotesquely large figures in the drawings for *Le Témoin*.

The following passage from a letter of the next year is relevant to his earliest painting style and all his later work:

Already I visualize quite different values of light and form—different possibilities of translation than therefore [sic]—but it seems nearly impossible to free oneself from the accepted reality of nature. That which is seen optically has to go through the process of *transformation* and *crystallization* to become a picture. . . .

The terms *transformation* and *crystallization,* underlined in the original, are noteworthy.

Feininger made some explicit comments about his earliest painting style in a letter to Churchill seven years later (March 13, 1913) in which he reviewed his development as a painter:

Having never painted before 1907 . . . it chanced that I never had fallen into Impressionism. My first pictures after I commenced in oil in April 1907 were caricatures in flat, decorative spots, after my drawings of such fantastic subject[s], made from time to time for my own relief. My vague ideal was to approach to the style of certain crude signboards, just barely escaping "rankness" as understood among "real" painters.

It is psychologically interesting that in this report to Churchill, the lover of impressionism, Feininger suppressed his own false start as an impressionist. But there is a description of it in Mrs. Moll's letter, and it was acknowledged by Feininger himself in the previously mentioned interview given to Peter Selz. In the interview he contrasted the impressionist manner, which he obviously could not learn quickly in landscape painting, with his figural style. He considered the latter his "primitive way"; it was similar to the treatment of figures in "cartoons and caricatures . . . like those in shooting galleries."

He again wrote of shooting gallery figures—the painted images cut from sheet metal in the booths at Parisian fairs—in a letter to his son Lux.[37] The painting *Street in Paris* (spring, 1909, Oeuvre Catalog No. 43) is similar in theme and treatment to *L'Exactitude,* the 1907 *Témoin* cartoon (reproduced by A. H. Barr under the title *Hurrying People*). Both show his shooting gallery figures.

Although Feininger made finer stylistic distinctions in the letter to Churchill, opaque color and simplified, poster-like style and treatment of subject are characteristic of his art from 1907 until May 1911. Then he went to Paris for the third time and came in contact with facet cubism.

At this point his style and technique changed considerably. But since there was little change in his choice of subject matter, the new works can be considered along with his earlier paintings. Feininger's Paris is unmistakably herself, yet neither his early work nor any of the later etchings ever repeat the impressionist vision of the city of light and gaiety. Instead there is a strangely quiet town in the earliest morning hours or just after the street lamps have been lit. The people seem scattered over the streets or are blown through them as though they had lost all control over their motions. Often one lonely character, a streetsweeper or lamplighter, wanders about like a phantom or appears from nowhere like an apparition. The architecture is mostly that of the old streets in the Latin Quarter or around the even older Tour St. Jacques. Although paintings with American motifs like *Old American Locomotive* (begun in 1914) become rarer now, they also possess this grotesque and macabre quality.

It is true that, as A. H. Barr put it, "Feininger's American contacts dwindled after he gave up illustration for easel painting in 1907."[38] But Feininger did exhibit in New York before the outbreak of the First World War. He had a few etchings in a show organized by a group he referred to as the *Photographische Gesellschaft* in the winter of 1913.[39]

This show was the immediate cause for a temporary renewal of the Churchill correspondence. Feininger twice referred to this exhibit in letters to Churchill. On February 3, 1913, he wrote about the artist Eduard A. Kramer, who is also mentioned in the Kortheuer letters: "You met my old friend Kramer in the exhibit, and he wrote about it and I asked him to give me your address, for it is many years since I've known where you are."[40] And on March 13, 1913: ". . . up to last Winter in New York at the

Photographische Gesellschaft's Exhibit, where you were, I have never yet sold a picture, etching or drawing."

Nevertheless he was gaining recognition from a circle of young artists and critics:

Now since about four weeks, I am becoming an object of attention to the very most gifted of the younger striving artists and critics here. Our quiet domicile (except for 3 rampant boys!) is suddenly become the favorite meeting place for a number of young people (compared to my late maturing self, just like you, old Al!) and every week one or the other brings in a new man who has become curious to know my work.

While he had made new friends through his art he had not forgotten his "old Al." Feininger's letter of February 3, 1913, in response to Churchill's note, reopened their correspondence:

God bless you, old fellow! Your dear, kind, generous words gave me the very greatest pleasure; no one would nor could write so but your dear self. As we get on in years (!) (I am myself already 41! and Al [you] must be about 52!)[41] we learn ever the better that there is no new friendship [which] can be so deep and enduring as the old, formed when we were young and could scarce imagine what golden enduring ties we entered into, to bless our riper years. . . .

Then he comes to the heart of the matter by explaining his present manner of painting, which he fears his friend may not approve because it has turned out to be different from Churchill's impressionism.

That my work is a (shall we call it a success? or does it merely 'attract attention'?), 'success' then—is somewhat of a surprise to me, . . . For, here in North Germany, there is little understanding for such and small encouragement extended to innovators, and I have long since learned to 'keep dark, lie low and watch' or rather "work." It is not given me, even if I so desired (which I do *not!*) to go the normal or beaten path in art—and it takes years and years of strenuous, unremitting and critical work and self-disciplining to put forth a new form. And for my conviction, Art is ever *new,* being Creation. I am painting exclusively since about

126

three years, although I keep up drawing for my own needs. But my work for the papers is at an end—there is no place for me there! The moment one goes one's own way, one is an outlaw. . . . Well I had about 14 years of it, and never dreaming that there was for me such a thing in the world as *art;* that was something quite outside of my treadmill existence. The awakening came like a wonder, to me. It is now some 5 years, since I commenced to work for myself.

This would place the beginning of his independence as an artist in the year 1908, as the letter of the next month (March 13) confirms:

In 1908 I came to have the opportunity of drawing out of doors all Summer and made very many notes, chiefly of figures, caricatures and experimenting with colored outlines and contrasting surfaces. The few figure notes dated 1908 will show you these and likewise that I followed motion very closely. [In] 1909 I first commenced to sketch landscape [in a style] still decorative, worshipful of van Gogh. [In] 1910 I had attained to greater rhythm, somewhat neglecting color, of which I felt perfectly sure.

The scrapbook contains an example of the kind of landscape Feininger mentions. It is a crayon drawing dated September, 1909. Flowing, undulating lines frame large, flat areas. It is certainly reminiscent of Van Gogh, but also has something of Gauguin's Brittany landscapes of 1886, especially in the choice of its brilliant colors.

During the terribly hot summer of 1906 the Feiningers had gone to Quiberville in Normandy, where he sketched a great deal. These sketches formed the basis for the oils of Normandy that he painted in 1909 after returning to Berlin. One of these landscapes, *Langueuil, Normandy,*[42] is indebted to Cézanne in the stylization of trees, although it has Feininger's hurrying people and his characteristic houses set at steep angles.

The next decisive step in Feininger's development as a painter occurred in 1911 when he encountered cubism. He wrote Churchill in the letter of March 13, 1913:

1911 had brought me to the critical state, where imitation of Nature is imminent, but in that Spring I had gone to Paris for two weeks and found the art world there agog with cubism—a thing I had never heard even mentioned before, but which I had already entirely striven after *for years*. So my studies after May 1911 (Paris) were, 'tis true, impressionistic but already *formulated*, more or less, and [in] 1912 I worked entirely independently, striving to wrest the secrets of atmospheric perspective and light and shade gradation, likewise rhythm and balance between various objects, from Nature. My cubism, to so miscall it, for it is the reverse of the French artists' claims, is based upon the principle of monumentality and *concentration* to the absolutest extreme possible of my visions, either compositional or before Nature. The French, as far as I have followed the works of Picasso, Friesz, Delaunay and Le Fauconnier, lose the concentration of vision and verge into chaotic dispersal of form and are actually reverting into a sort of neo-neo-impressionism.

Two of Feininger's statements here are of special importance. First, that he had intuitively striven for many years toward something he had called in previous letters "transformation," "formulation," even "crystallization" of nature, before he came in actual contact with French cubism in Paris about May of 1911; second, that his cubism was based more on concentration than on analysis. He insisted that the cubist crystallization process in his works was positive and constructive, not dissolving and destructive.

Today it is apparent that the facet cubism of a Picasso leads through analysis, or breaking down of the object in nature, to a new cohesiveness and consolidation of form and that therefore neither Feininger's distinction nor his implied criticism is valid. There is, however, a difference between the manner and degree of the analytical process in his own paintings and in French cubism. Often the French totally dismantle the original object and so give the impression of its atomization or destruction, in which Feininger sees a "neo-neo-impressionism."

To many viewers the starting point in nature may become lost and the whole thereby unintelligible, while in Feininger's early cubist paintings, like the *Bicyclists* of 1912 or the *Sidewheeler* of 1913,[43] the object is always present and clearly recognizable even to the uninitiated viewer. It retains its cohesive totality in spite of its organization into facets resembling glass splinters. The mirror of the picture plane may be splintered, yet the represented object maintains its aggregated existence on the cracked but not disarranged shards; in French cubist painting the object may be explosively fragmentized and scattered all over the picture plane.

Lux Feininger describes the result in a very similar way in his article *Two Painters*, which came to the author's attention after the foregoing lines were written.

Indeed the first indications of his own sign language appeared before the formulation of cubist ideals in Paris. I should rather incline to the idea of a parallel development—in some principal features, such as the interpenetration of crystalline forms in invertible perspective, strikingly alike—with different aims. Lyonel Feininger's aim was a deeper more searching penetration of landscape, figure and architecture than the conventional means of linear and atmospheric perspective offered; but he was never interested in breaking up form.

His forms are not broken up: they are rather built up. What we see, to continue the metaphor, are the joints of component parts; not fracture lines of a cracking structure. The geometrical plane, for the most part rectilinear, although there are important compositions in circular and spiralling forms, whether pure or derived, is the unifying factor in his compositions; carrier of formal and color ideas both.[44]

The subjects in the two examples of Feininger's early cubist phase, *Bicyclists* and *Sidewheeler,* are memories of his American childhood, quite different from such familiar props of early French cubism as guitars, pipes, and newspapers. Parallels between his subjects and those of the contemporary Italian futurists are more evident. Feininger and the futurists share the climate of feeling in a technically oriented society; both find fascination in the dynamism of metal vehicles. In 1912 futurist paintings and sculpture were exhibited in Berlin at the *Sturm* gallery, where Feininger certainly saw them.

Feininger's claim that from 1912 he worked to wrest from nature its secrets of atmospheric perspective, light and shade, rhythm and balance, indicates that he did not superimpose a cubist formula on nature. Rather he tried to discover its inherent laws, its structure—an aim similar to Cézanne's. Yet he was especially concerned with the intangibles—space and atmosphere, and the gradation of light and shade.

His formulations at the end of the same letter reveal the spiritual values he found in these elements. But before evaluating these qualities let us look at the artistic situation in the Paris of 1911 as Feininger, an active participant, knew it.

The first impressive exhibit of the cubists as a group was in the *Salon d'Automne* of 1911. They also had their own room in the exhibit of *Indépendants,* among them Gleizes, Metzinger, Le Fauconnier, Gris, Léger. Delaunay had been shown in the *Indépendants* of 1910, the year he started his series of the Eiffel Tower. His subjects were then divided between the Eiffel Tower and the Gothic (his paintings of St. Séverin are from 1909). His work appealed to Feininger, as it did to the two German artists Franz Marc and August Macke, who met Delaunay when they visited Paris. Feininger met him at the studio of Richard Goetz,[45] formerly Whistler's Paris quarters. Delaunay later formulated a theory about his own art, his so-called Orphic Cubism of 1912, which laid particular stress on prismatic light. Its printed formulation was "too quasi-scientific" for Feininger. In a letter to Julia from Weimar, September 25, 1913, he explained:

> I am afraid I do not fit into this company either, though they at least are after true forming (*Gestaltung*). But for the time being, they pluck to pieces, and I strain in the opposite direction: concentration, monumentality.[46]

Henri Le Fauconnier (1881–1946), whose name appeared last on Feininger's list, was second only to Delaunay as a chief link between the French and German artists. In 1910 he had taught in Munich, where he had been a member of the *New Artists' League* (*Neue Künstlervereinigung*), a parent organization of the

Blaue Reiter. Othon Friesz (1879–1949) had exhibited with the Fauves in 1905 and was a follower of Matisse. He had stayed in Munich in 1909. Friesz was less a cubist than any of the artists Feininger mentioned in his letter.

It is probably intentional that Feininger put Picasso's name in the first place when, in his letter to Churchill, he enumerated the French cubists whose art he felt to be so different from his own. In 1911, after a summer in Céret with Braque, Picasso reached the peak of analytical dismembering in his paintings. *Man with Pipe* (in the Fogg Art Museum, Cambridge, Massachusetts) goes even beyond such portraits as *Wilhelm Uhde* and *D. H. Kahnweiler* of the previous year.

Feininger, who resumed his relations with Pascin and the circle at the Dôme, stayed in Paris for only two weeks—just long enough to learn the latest events in the art world. But he was represented in the avant-garde shows. He had six paintings in the *Salon des Indépendants*[47] and two in the *Salon d'Automne*.

Charlotte Teller[48] records Matisse's great admiration for the paintings which Feininger exhibited in Paris. Almost as if in reciprocation, there is a slight influence of the leader of the Fauvists in Feininger's work; for example, in a *Still Life* of 1912.[49]

In spite of the great differences which Feininger saw between his own cubist paintings and those of the French, some of his portraits, like the *Self Portrait with Viaduct* of 1915,[50] are at least superficially reminiscent of such relatively restrained Picassos as the *Wilhelm Uhde*. The most cubistic of these paintings is the *Head in Architecture* of 1917 (Oeuvre Catalog No. 169), yet the integration of the head and the architectural planes are strongly characteristic of Feininger's personal style.

Parisian galleries exhibited primitive art, including African and South Pacific sculpture, and progressive artists began to collect it. In a letter to Churchill of uncertain date Feininger comments: "Don't mix up the possibilities of art proper and of *decorative* art. The barbarian art is the best decorative art, tho the two combined *decoratively* are noble."

This rather cryptic statement probably means that decorative values alone (exemplified to a European by "barbarian" art) are not sufficient. They must be allied with content to become meaningful for a Western viewer. Feininger's own art reflects his commitment to this concept; in it he combines cubist technique with romantic content.

Feininger's short stay in Paris in the spring of 1911 was his initiation into the world of advanced art. After his return to Germany he was increasingly a force in progressive art movements. Only then did he establish real contact with his German contemporaries, as Peter Selz has pointed out.[51] He met Heckel, Mueller, Pechstein and Kubin; Schmidt-Rottluff invited him to join the *Brücke* group in 1912 and painted his portrait in 1915.[52]

From 1909 through 1912 Feininger had paintings in the exhibitions of the Berlin Secession. The Secession was a mildly progressive group controlled by the German impressionists Liebermann and Corinth. In contrast to it, Herwarth Walden's *Herbst* (autumn) *Salon* was radical from its outset and a challenge to established taste. Alfred Kubin (born 1877 in Leitmeritz, Bohemia) became Feininger's close friend; it was he who got Franz Marc to invite Feininger to exhibit with the *Blaue Reiter* at Walden's First German Autumn Salon in Berlin in 1913.[53]

Feininger was not a full-fledged member of either of the radical groups, the *Blaue Reiter* or Walden's *Sturm*. The *Blaue Reiter* had been formed in Munich, and since Feininger lived in Berlin, he had no part in the preparation of the book which gave its name to the group, nor was he represented at its first exhibit in 1911 at the Thannhauser gallery in Munich. According to L. Schreyer,[54] his four paintings at the 1913 Autumn Salon were not hung with those of the *Blaue Reiter*, but in another room. His friendship with Kubin rested on personal feeling rather than partisan association, although Kubin's fantastic and demonic pen drawings no doubt had a strong appeal to the imaginative Feininger.

Feininger always avoided noisy display. In the letter to Churchill of March 13, 1913, half a year before the show organized by Walden, Feininger wrote of "that cheapest of all renown, publicity! . . . I give not a 'tinker's damn' for public approval. . . ."

More than any other in the entire correspondence, this letter reveals Feininger's ideas about art and the artist's function in society. Toward the end of its eight pages he tells how his style evolved from childhood impressions, even from his earliest drawings, through cartooning to his latest paintings.

I 'hark back' since [through the] years, to my childish impressions; the monumentality, the freedom from conventional perspective trammeling the phantasy; all were strongest in the child, and it is surely for the ripening man, to best realize them. . . . [As a caricaturist] I was invariably berated and threatened *with loss of position* for the very traits which make me an artist of original power! When not working (which is always) and when working mentally only, I play Bach and Buxtehude on my Estey Harmonium: Music is as much my life as air and creating in paint. My pictures are ever nearing closer the *Synthesis of the fugue;* not one necessary spot . . . which will not bear analysis with reference to the whole. That is my *formal* aim. Have you thought over this primal element of *enduring* art?
Cubism is a synthesis, but may easily be degraded into mechanism. I had the courage to start out absolutely mechanically to work through to the *living* form: my 'cubism' (again falsely so called, call it rather, if it must have a name, "prism-ism," although that is but one element of it) is *visionary* not physical.

This is the most important statement that Feininger made about his art in the letters to Churchill. It encompasses his later work at the Bauhaus as it harks back to his American childhood. It further reveals that his work as a cartoonist for American and European papers, which he now regarded as a "grind of fourteen years," was nevertheless the second root from which sprang the liberties he took as a free artist. And what a happy choice is "prismism" to describe his individual form of cubism! Twenty-eight years later, in the catalog for the Feininger exhibition in Berlin, Ludwig Thormaehlen suggested another word—*prismatism.*
Most interesting, and mentioned for the first time in these letters, is the explanation of his cubism in terms of music. In

Feininger's art, music (especially the Bach fugue) is related to color, light, perspective, and space. All are paths to the intangibly divine. Therefore solid substances become more and more dematerialized in his oils and watercolors. Feininger purifies existence through light.

In an article in *Das Junge Deutschland*,[55] Theodore Däubler, one of the outstanding German expressionist poets, called Feininger the "clearest crystal-former" (*Klarster Kristalliker*). And he went on: "But the crystals *breathe*, grow, live and love!" Däubler did not overlook the fact that Feininger was not only a visionary but belonged to the modern world of constructions, which the poet saw epitomized in America: "In this respect German-American. Essentially modern-constructive (Darin Deutsch-Amerikaner. Durchaus modern-konstruierend)."

As was his habit with any German criticism of his work,[56] Feininger sent this article—more poem than prose—to Churchill. During 1913 he also continued to send many small drawings, which Churchill then pasted into the scrapbook. They are far too numerous to describe, ranging from the cartoon-like *Figure-Motion Studies* (some of them in crayon) done in 1908 in Heringsdorf at the Baltic Sea, to the prismatic *Trees* and *Thuringian Villages* of 1913.

Three characteristic pencil drawings which present steps in his development are here reproduced. Feininger referred to them as thumbnail sketches. The first (fig. 45, dated "Sat. Sept. 11, 09") was one of many he made the first summer after his return to Germany from Paris. In the stress on the oblique plane of the village road rising from the foreground, it is still indebted to compositional devices he employed in his cartoons and early paintings. The undulating motion of the trees recalls Van Gogh and Gauguin.

The second (fig. 46, Heringsdorf; Wednesday, September 13, 1911) illustrates one of Feininger's favorite motifs. A group of strollers are silhouetted against a sea which pales away to a sailboat on the horizon. This now becomes a frequent subject in Feininger's art, recurring even in his last paintings.

45. Village street, near Heringsdorf. Crayon sketch. 1909.

46. Strollers on Heringsdorf beach. Crayon sketch. 1911.

The drawing of a village street in Thuringia near Weimar (dated June 23, 1913) done in green crayon is an excellent early example of "prismism" (fig. 47). The slant of the two hurrying people who are reduced to mere signs is echoed and contrasted in the angles of an architecture seemingly built of light rays. It is prophetic of Feininger's later work.

The generous selection of drawings and the two very long letters of February and March 1913 were not only Feininger's means of telling his friend what had happened during the long interruption in their correspondence: it was also a sincere attempt to convince Churchill that the path that led him to cubism was the right one. Feininger must have known that this was a difficult task. When he begs Churchill at the end of the first letter, "Above all, never old Al, think me a 'faddist,' " it seems that Feininger fears to be thought just that. He continues:

I possessed the elements of so-called *cubism* before I had ever heard of such a thing or seen a cubistic painting.—My work of 5 and more years ago shows already the tendency towards a new and absolutely *personal perspective;* as to color—well, when I was but a mere hobbledehoy at the 'Akademie' in 89, you called me a 'colorist.'

In 1924, Churchill, by then a college professor and museum director, wrote his only article about Feininger. Called *Lyonel Feininger, Woodcut-Artist,*[57] this brief statement supports the assumption that Churchill was not fully in sympathy with Feininger's cubism. He introduces the artist as "an American boy," for he had known Feininger at art school in Berlin, and to Churchill he is "still a boy" now become "one of the leading artists of Germany." He explains that the war has delayed Feininger's fame in America. He deals with Feininger's woodcut technique in some detail but fails to say anything about his style. Then he quotes from one of Feininger's letters: "I deny being anything at all with an 'ism' attached to it."[58] The article ends rather lamely and apologetically:

47. Thuringian village scene. Crayon sketch. 1913.

One may not be able to follow the artist in everything he does. One may not believe at all in the aesthetic theory which underlies his effect. But it is impossible for one who knows his work not to recognize his gift of color, and of form, and his seriousness of purpose.

This was written ten years after the correspondence of the friends had been interrupted again, this time by World War I. It was not to be resumed until some months after the armistice, with a last letter to Churchill. Feininger had written in the letter of Feb. 3, 1913: "Perhaps I may in a year or two come over to the States, after 26 years' absence." So the war also prevented the realization of his plan to visit his homeland.

Lothar Schreyer's *Erinnerungen an Sturm und Bauhaus* (*Memoirs of Sturm and Bauhaus*)[59] reveals that Feininger, as an enemy alien, was placed in semi-internment near Berlin after America entered the war. Thanks to Herwarth Walden, who had shown Feininger's work at his Sturm Gallery, and who had connections with the Foreign Office, Feininger was allowed occasional visits outside.

Schreyer, the painter, stage designer, and later, master at the Bauhaus, met Feininger at a tea at Walden's home in Berlin. It was the time of Feininger's first one-man show, held in September of 1917 at the Sturm Gallery. The expressionist poets Rudolf Bluemner, Theodor Däubler, and Adolf Knoblauch[60] were also in attendance. One result of this meeting was an exchange of letters between Knoblauch and Feininger.[61] In this correspondence Feininger again cites his American childhood as the source of his art. Here, in translation, is a passage from one of his letters to Knoblauch:

Image is symbol! Over and over again I try to penetrate into the meaning of great symbols, such as bridge, house, church, tower, and to paint them. . . . Church, mill, bridge, house and cemetery have filled me since childhood with deeply pious sentiments. They are all symbols, but I became fully aware that this is so only after this war started, and I know now why I must paint them over and over again. Memories are rooted in childhood days.

They last through one's life! The future is yearning and longing—and the present: work.

Feininger's 1917 show at the *Sturm* Gallery consisted of forty-six paintings and sixty-five watercolors and drawings. It was followed a month before the armistice by another in Munich at the Galerie Hans Goltz's *48. Ausstellung Neue Kunst (Fortieth Exhibit of New Art)*. Both shows were overshadowed by the threatened collapse of Imperial Germany and breathed the spirit of the troubled times.[62] *Riot (Aufruhr)* was the subject of a grotesque pen drawing of 1909;[63] a closely related oil of 1910, *Great Revolution (Grosse Revolution)*,[64] belonged to a group Feininger called *Masquerade Pictures (Mummenschanz-Bilder)*. What he represented in them as a farce, a hilarious and somewhat drunken masquerade of reality, occurred in bloody earnest a decade later.

After the war, Feininger was one of the first to be called by Walter Gropius to teach at the Bauhaus at Weimar. Feininger taught at the now world-famous school for five years. For a time he was form master of the printing and graphics workshop; later he taught painting (he was painter in residence until 1924 in Weimar, from 1925 to 1933 in Dessau). The school was closed by the Nazis after it moved to Berlin, and Feininger's work was included in the exhibitions of "degenerate art" in 1937.

Soon after arriving at the Bauhaus, Feininger tried to reestablish contact with Churchill. His letter, addressed to Churchill's wife Marie, is decorated with a small woodcut. It is an example of his latest work and a consoling message to his friends. A high tower surmounts houses under the moon and stars. In style it is similar to the *Cathedral of Socialism* he had designed for the *First Bauhaus Manifesto* in 1919.

We take leave of the friendship of Feininger and Churchill with excerpts from Feininger's last letter to Marie, written August 22, 1920.

No word from old Al! and nothing I have written him seems to have reached him. It is the same with all my letters to my father, in New York and the different friends in the States although I had mail regularly registered. I am very unhappy about it and it increases greatly the mental horror I am going through for many years; but most especially since the so called *end* of the war.

After thanking Marie Churchill for clothing and tobacco he ends the letter with a moving appeal for suffering Europe:

May these lines only reach you! The world is *murdering* Europe, more surely than during the war: We are in *desperate* condition and *no outlook* whatever for years to come. How cruel mankind has become; how cruel *Nations* are grown! Yet, individuals are kind; and quite *helpless!* It is all "Politics," the worst of Devilment.

We are relatively well, more fortunate therein than many, many tens of Millions; but we shall very probably never fully recover [from] the effects of these years.

God bless you, and try to give me Al's address! I have a vague hope of his turning up, some time in September, as he wrote in May.

Truly yours   old friend Leo

THE FLOWERING OF FANTASY

V

Prints, Watercolors, and Paintings of the Later Years;
World War I, Bauhaus, and Return to America, 1912–56

Feininger's ghosts often look *almost* human. In his political cartoons they appear as sinister forces of bigotry and reaction. In other magazine drawings they might be New Year's spooks rising from alcoholic fumes. Often they bedevil technical contrivances or sit at the wheels of fantastic yet prophetic mechanisms. These goblins were familiar to him since his childhood; then he could imagine them lurking in the shadows of the El, riding in trains, or wearing striped prisoners' uniforms.

They come again to his early paintings. Here they are flat and colorful shooting gallery figures dressed in American sport clothes and Biedermeier top hats; or street cleaners, canal sweepers, lamplighters, or gossips. Or they might be spirits who possess mobs rioting for a ridiculous cause. They can behave like ordinary citizens, but they always have a sinister aura, like characters in the tales of Hoffmann. They haunt narrow, crooked evening streets dimly lit by old-fashioned lamps which glow but shed no light. It is a setting like the old parts of Paris, small medieval German towns or the scenery for *The Cabinet of Dr. Caligari,* the German film that followed these works a decade later.

Streets, houses, and even modern machines fall under the spell. One of Feininger's earliest graphic non-cartoon projects was a *Cycle of Locomotives* in colored lithographs. He finished only a few. One of them, *Decrepit Locomotive* of 1906,[1] is a ghostly vintage machine that still manages to retain a dreadful temper. Another locomotive, this time in dry point, evokes an entirely different mood (fig. 48). The whimsical locomotive (which

143

48. *Lokomotive*. Drypoint. 1906.

first appeared in a "Wee Willie Winkie" strip) rushes through the night, its huge headlight-eyes turned watchfully toward the steep embankment. A year earlier, Feininger had planned a series to be called *Old Towns* that would also have had a magical, humanized atmosphere. Feininger's fantasy pervades the early etchings, especially those of 1911 like *Anglers, Disparagers,* and *Dream City,* whose smallness lends them an intimate quality. They are signed *Einoel Leinfinger,* the artist's whimsical double. Their subjects resemble those of the *Masquerade Pictures,* but the outlines are nervous, almost scribbled—in contrast to the sharp rendering in the paintings.

Some of Feininger's contemporaries brought a similar feeling to their work. The technique of his friends Jules Pascin and Francis Christopher was akin to his, but the art of the Austrian writer and illustrator Alfred Kubin displays the greatest affinity with Feininger's fantasy style. Kubin sent Feininger his book *Die andere Seite* (Munich, 1908) whose text and illustrations make it an outstanding example of macabre fantasy. The figures in Kubin's black-and-white drawings sometimes wear Biedermeier costumes, but there the resemblance in subject ends. As Hess has rightly remarked,[2] Feininger always avoided horror, torture, and the nightmarish scenes which abound in Kubin's work. Hess has published excerpts from letters the two exchanged in which Feininger acknowledges that he lives "a little" in Kubin's "mysterious country."

In another letter Feininger says that both of them are "not disposed ever to resort to pure abstraction." This is true even in the woodcuts he began to make in 1918. Possibly because of the demands of the medium, they are more stylized than his other graphics. But even they are never fully abstract. The figures of his etchings appear again—tall, top-hatted men with elfin companions—but in silhouette, like the black paper cutouts his wife Julia once liked to make.

There is a threatening undertone, a spirit of conspiracy concealed by impassivity, in the men silently and unemotionally watching the arrival of the *Fishing Fleet* (F 1884)[3] like ghosts certain of catching their victims.

Feininger made most of his early woodcuts during the turbulent final months of the war and the succeding period of revolution, when the family often went hungry. It was difficult to get paints. Perhaps this explains his concentration on woodcuts, whose black and white express so well the somberness of the times. Walden published many of the smaller ones in his radical magazine, *Sturm*. At this time Feininger began to make his woodcut *Letterheads*, condensed versions of favorite subjects.

Besides themes inspired by the chaotic situation in Germany, Feininger worked on subjects recalled from past years, such as *Houses in Paris* (F 1861), or even from his childhood. *Virtuoso* (F 1961), a woodcut of 1919 printed on yellow paper (fig. 2), recalls one of the *Concerts* he drew as a boy. The scene has the character of a puppet show: the bow of the virtuoso is suddenly jerked upward, the pianist pounds frantically on the piano. The violinist stands on the edge of a coffin-like stage, the pianist and piano seem to be sliding downwards.

Railroad Viaduct (F 1941), also from 1919, is perhaps the outstanding work of Feininger's eerie style of this period. Unusually large (13⅛ inches by 16⅞ inches), it was probably one of the first prints Feininger made after he became form master at the Bauhaus printing and graphics workshop. Here childhood fears and excitements are combined. A rickety early-American train chugs over a high viaduct. The tall houses seem to have been shaken to a slant. Some figures look like clowns; others, as small as insects, are more like ghouls. In *Railroad Viaduct* Feininger approaches the style of Paul Klee, whose work he already knew. Yet Klee's art did not exert a direct influence on this print or any of the other products of Feininger's Bauhaus period. It is rather that the terse, visual shorthand of Feininger's woodcuts and his increasingly philosophic humor ally his vision with Klee's. These two, who were colleagues and close friends at the Bauhaus in Weimar, had an affinity of style and imagination.

The style of the early woodcuts persists in Feininger's later art, in paintings as well as woodcuts. Paintings of 1940 and 1941— *At the Seaside* (Oeuvre Catalog 392), *Anglers* (Oeuvre Catalog 393), and *Night Express* (Oeuvre Catalog 411)—all recall the prints of 1918 and 1919 in both style and subject.

The early woodcuts were an important element in the disciplining of Feininger's style. In his paintings after 1922 the human figure is totally subordinated to and dwarfed by the majestic architecture of light, color, and space. This is especially true of the Beach pictures, where people seem to be mere compositional accents or symbols of human smallness and insignificance. The now often luminous silhouettes in these works are still related to their predecessors in the woodcuts in their flatness, angularity and puppet-like appearance. And these figures watch in the same silent way. They turn their backs to the onlooker and so become mediators between him and the world beyond the picture plane. Like the woodcut figures they are not quite real: although they stand in light, they belong to the world of shadows.

These unreal beings continue to inhabit Feininger's later and more active figural scenes, such as the two paintings of 1933, *Bathers* (Oeuvre Catalog 353) and *Figures at the Seashore* (Oeuvre Catalog 357), and the 1950 painting, *Wanderer by the Sea II* (Oeuvre Catalog 492). Alfred Hentzen writes in the preface to the catalog for the Feininger Memorial Exhibition of 1961:

> Feininger never abrogated his early work. The grotesque creations of his fantasy . . . never disappear from his work. They become small in size in the classical work of the Bauhaus years, but they survive into the last period where they recur in small watercolors, transfigured and transformed but always hovering between melancholy and gaiety.

Goblins find their way into the drawings and watercolors of the twenties, especially the informal works like his pictorial "Thanks to Friends" which Hans Hess reproduces from his father's guest book.[4] One is titled *On the Shortest Day of the Year, Dec. 21, 1922* (*Am kürzesten Tage, 21, XII. 22*). Ghosts roam the silent, frozen

49. Pen and watercolor letterheads. 1951.
a) *Ill-Tempered Clavier.*

b) *"Tristesse," "Lamentation," "Wehklage."*

c) *Choir-rehearsal.*

world, while little round-headed trolls with ridiculously solemn top hats crowd together on an arched stone bridge in a wintry forest of lofty pines under the new moon. Feininger subtitled the watercolor *Little Ghosts, Friendly Ones* (*Gespensterchen, Gutartige*).

Eighteen years later in America he translated this small watercolor into an oil called *Spook I* [Oeuvre Catalog 395]. Earlier he made another watercolor in the Hess guest book (June 27, 1921), *People on the Boardwalk.* In the painting, a procession of twelve trolls of varying heights and wearing red coats and top hats, winds its way on a precariously narrow walk built on red piles far out in the sea.

These brilliantly-colored watercolors have the lines of Feininger's early etchings—almost scribbled, like children's drawings, which was what Feininger called them.[5] Their nervousness and tremulousness contrast with the neat "surgical cuts" which Lothar Schreyer observed in the majority of his work.

The prankish but benign goblins do not seem to be fully corporealized; they give the impression that they will disappear before one's eyes before they have ever fully existed. These little ghosts reappear in the late watercolors *Spook Afraid of Himself* (1945)[6] and *Heat II* (date uncertain);[7] in *Heat II* they melt away beneath the relentless sun of a summer day in New York. And they can be found in the *Letterheads* of the fifties with which Feininger decorated his letters to Laurence. Three examples: *Ill-Tempered Klavier* (without date), *Tristesse, Lamentation, Wehklage* (December 10, 1951), and *Choir Rehearsal* (December 16, 1951)—are reproduced in fig. 49a, b, c.

Feininger developed these playthings of passing whims and idle hours into components of serious works in oil and watercolor, including some of the most profound creations of his last decades in America. In *Blind Musician on the Beach* (1942, Oeuvre Catalog 422) two of these ghost-like creatures—one red, one white— follow a ghostly flame: the pathetic, blind figure with a guitar, dressed all in red, who feels his way with a cane as he sings his song of loneliness and madness to the ocean and to the boats riding the waves like phantoms.

Hess rightly calls *Blind Musician on the Beach* one of Feininger's great figural compositions. It bears an affinity to an earlier painting, *Red Fiddler* (1934, Oeuvre Catalog 359). Both works are milestones in Feininger's development as an artist and as a man. In contrast to the jagged, scribbly lines of *Blind Musician* (which was based on a watercolor of 1915), *Red Fiddler* is done in Feininger's usual line cuts. The two paintings are related in color (the fearful reds) and subject (ghost musicians). The figures in *Red Fiddler* hark back to the shooting gallery forms of Feininger's earliest paintings.

Red Fiddler is a highly ambiguous picture. A demonic figure from one of Hoffmann's tales, such as "Kapellmeister Kreisler," infects its Biedermeier world; but it may also be viewed as Feininger's covert statement of his reaction to the Hitler regime: a fiendishly artful melody leading to destruction. The *Red Fiddler* is the devil himself; the witch or procuress shadowing the doll-like young beauty and the sinister old man are types of the common life which thoughtlessly goes on, easily duped and persuaded. Whatever the specific interpretation, it is an ominous picture, comparable to Thomas Mann's nightmarish vision of medieval Germany. The parallels between Feininger's *Red Fiddler* and a passage from Mann's 1945 essay "Germany and the Germans"[8] are indeed close. It is not only in the somber medieval silhouette of an old Nordic town with its crow-gabled houses and towers that the two artists concur creatively, but also in its pathological and demonic characters.

This eerie painting, with its demonic fiddler accompanying Germany's inevitable *Danse Macabre,* marks the end of Feininger's German years.

Feininger had never cut his ties with America. He retained his citizenship even after he knew that this would subject him to repressive regulations during the First World War. His letters to Kortheuer, Churchill, and Knoblauch often reveal his strong feeling for his homeland, and there is ample evidence of it in the years after 1920, when his correspondence with Churchill ended. He always remained American in appearance and speech. After visiting him at his Berlin studio in 1917, Charlotte Teller commented, "Feininger is an American—a typical American."[9] Ten years later, A. H. Barr, Jr. talked with him at the Bauhaus in Dessau. Listening to Feininger's speech, Barr was "surprised and fascinated . . . by its strange purity of accent and antiquated slang . . . we were talking with an American who, through some time-machine miracle, had been preserved unchanged since the 1880's."[10] In 1924 Feininger wrote a letter to his wife (which Barr quotes) giving his reaction to an American film, *The Westbound Limited,* whose subject had fascinated him from childhood on.

A wonderful railroad film taken in the Rockies. I was quite carried away. . . . My American childhood had got me and I became acutely conscious of the poisonous atmosphere in which one is living here and that I too am a free American and the country across the ocean still my own land.

When he wrote these lines, Feininger had not yet visited the setting for the film, but he would imagine what such regions of America were like—he called a watercolor of April 3, 1923, *Evening at Lake Michigan (Abend am Michigan).*[11]

He was always interested in American art and artists. In 1913 he became familiar with the work of Marsden Hartley when they both exhibited at the Berlin Autumn Salon (they met a few years later). Feininger, never very sympathetic to expressionism, was as Barr observed, "less influenced by German art than was Hartley." His art had more in common with the works of Demuth and Marin; it is a pity he did not meet them when they were in Europe. Both Barr and E. P. Richardson[13] have placed Feininger with "precisionists of the twenties, American artists who adapted the cubist language of line and plane to the poetry of light and nature." (The words are Richardson's.)

In 1924 the Blue Four was formed in Weimar.[14] The four were Feininger, two friends from the Bauhaus, Wasilly Kandinsky and Paul Klee, and Alexei von Jawlensky, who had been loosely associated with the *Blue Rider*. (Through the efforts of Galka Scheyer, there were shows in New York, Chicago,[15] on the West Coast [1926] and in Mexico.) When Feininger exhibited with the group, he was invariably considered a European artist. It was only later that the affinities with his American contemporaries became apparent.

In 1929 the Museum of Modern Art in New York included seven of his paintings in a show called *Nineteen Living Americans*. They were received coldly.

Feininger always hoped to return to the land of his birth. He often mentioned this in his letters to Kortheuer and Churchill. At the time of the show at the Museum of Modern Art he seriously considered it. But he thought he would feel uprooted after so many years in Germany. Eight years later he finally came, a fugitive from the Nazis, who had defamed and banned his work.[16] He first went "tentatively" in 1936 to teach a summer course at Mills College in California. When the ship docked in New York harbor, Kortheuer, along with another old friend from his boyhood, was there to greet him. That autumn he returned to Berlin, where he made the final decision to emigrate with his family. He arrived in New York on June 17, 1937. He was sixty-five years old and nearly penniless. One might echo the words Churchill wrote under some drawings of 1908 when he began a new life as a painter: "Feininger starts all over again."

Now, as he vigorously undertook a third reconstruction of his life, Feininger's art entered its last, and to many, its finest phase.

He received a friendly reception in America. "I met with kindness and good will all around," he said.[17] He took an apartment high in a modern building and set up a tiny but neat studio there. In 1938 he was commissioned to paint the murals in the Marine Transportation and Masterpieces of Art buildings at the New York World's Fair. Many exhibits in museums and galleries followed. Among the most significant were those at the Detroit Institute of Art and at the Russell A. Alger House in Grosse Pointe,

Michigan, in 1941; the Museum of Modern Art in 1944 (a joint exhibit with Marsden Hartley); Boston's Institute of Contemporary Art, with Jacques Villon, 1949; and the Cleveland Museum of Art in 1951. His works were eagerly sought for public and private collections. In the West Coast painter Mark Tobey he found a close and understanding friend.[18] He spent the summer months teaching or sketching outside New York. Each summer from 1938 to 1944 he lived in Falls Village, Connecticut. In the summer of 1945 he was at Black Mountain College in North Carolina and at Stockbridge, Massachusetts. He returned to Stockbridge the next three years, was at Center Moriches on Long Island in 1949 and Cambridge and Plymouth, Massachusetts, in 1950 and 1952. He spent the summer of 1951 at Gropius' house at South Lincoln, Massachusetts. In 1953 he was in New Haven, Connecticut, with Joseph Albers, and back at Plymouth. He came back to Stockbridge in the summers of 1954 and 1955.

Feininger's teaching and his exhibitions had a great influence on young American painters. In the course of his teaching at Mills and Black Mountain he became familiar with American college life. Occasionally one of the whimsical little ghouls he drew on greeting cards for his family or friends would be wearing a mortarboard![19]

His range of American subjects widened. He made many pictures of Manhattan's skyscrapers and warehouses, most often in the enchantment of quiet, starry nights. There are views of San Francisco, the Pacific Northwest, the Yukon, rural Connecticut, and the great rivers and lakes. But another factor in the growth of Feininger's art was still more significant than his enrichment of subject. It was the recovery of the longings, excitements and even the fears of his youth.

As early as 1916 he had written:

> The older I get the more I am concerned with the problems of awareness, recollection and nostalgia. It seems obvious that the artist must strive to answer these questions, for longing is the impulse and mainspring of creative achievement.[20]

Now, after fifty years, the artist returned to the scenes of his boyhood. They were greatly changed.

The gigantic skyscrapers that dominated Manhattan had all been built while he was away. He found that only a few old buildings still stood near the place where he was born. From his studio windows he saw the roofs of factories and warehouses; he could even catch glimpses of boats on the East River until new buildings shut off that view of childhood delights. Once he made a sentimental journey to Sharon, Connecticut, where he had spent some of his early years. An old man in a rocking chair still remembered his father's virtuoso violin playing in the village church.

The old man returned to America but the child in him still saw ghosts—the old American trains still rattled over the elevated. *Railroad Train* (1941, Oeuvre Catalog 407) and *Night Express* (1941, Oeuvre Catalog 411) are re-created from memories. *Phantom Ships* of his youthful fantasies sail the Atlantic (1942, Oeuvre Catalog 420). In *Adventure II* (1940, Oeuvre Catalog 402) a man hurries past the apparition of a seductive woman who personifies the lure of the city on a hot and humid summer night. In a later painting the moon creates an even ghostlier phantom of another temptress and projects it on the high walls of the city. This time the wraith is not black but white, spun from the silver threads of the moon. The English title is *Moonwake* (1945, Oeuvre Catalog 460; the German, *Im Kielwasser des Mondes*).

Ghosts still appear under the arches of the viaduct; in *Spook II* (1941, Oeuvre Catalog 408) the female wears a light dress, the male is in the guise of an old man in black with a cane.

The artist meets a ghost from the past as he strolls along the night streets of *Mann-a-Hatta* (the original Indian name Feininger used for the title of a painting of 1952, Oeuvre Catalog 517). It is the black-clad man with the cane again; he is a solemn gentleman, wearing a top hat and a cravat long out of fashion—a memory of the dress worn by the men Feininger served as a Wall Street messenger when he was a boy.

In *Crépuscule* of 1952 (Oeuvre Catalog 521) the ghostly

wanderer with the cane has been transmuted into a white, hardly definable spot of light, a symbol of resignation or perhaps of hope. Silence and loneliness are still wrapped around him as he walks between night and day, darkness and light, which fight their eternal battle on the walls of a New York canyon. But it seems as if light, opalescent between soft greens and blues, triumphs over dark shadows.

The struggle with ghosts is still discernable in two of the most profound and moving works of Feininger's old age—*Vanishing Hour* (1952, Oeuvre Catalog 514) and *Shadow of Dissolution* (1953, Oeuvre Catalog 532). They are the ultimate creations of his fantasy, expressing the recognition that everything passes, is destroyed by time—a law which even ghosts must obey.

Feininger fully realized his characteristic vision in the paintings and watercolors of the decade before his death in 1956. Objects are still recognizable, but they are merely suggested with an airy transparency that indicates the artist's deeply religious quest for the formless, the limitless, and the unrenderable. As in Cézanne's last, breath-like watercolors of Mont Sainte-Victoire, what remains of reality is merely a colored veil beyond which one may catch glimpses of a loftier creation. As Feininger wrote to Barr in 1944, he had found his true country at last:

> In Germany I was 'der Amerikaner'; here in my native land I was sometimes classified and looked upon as a German painter. . . . but what is the artist, if not connected with the Universe?[21]

In her foreword to *A Memorial Exhibit from Fort Worth Collections* (1956) Cynthia Brant describes Feininger in his last years.

> The artist had almost the same effect on one as did his pictures. He was quiet, precise, and without embellishment in both manner and dress. He seemed gentle and modest—almost to the point of shyness. There was an air of energy and quickness about him, not held in check so much as directed.[22]

Photographs taken at this time often show him standing before a background of one of his paintings, such as *Stars above the*

Town. In a curious way he seems to merge with his work. His art may be likened to a journey through a city. High above the streets with their strange, tiny, often comic men—and ghosts— higher than the tallest buildings, a slender viaduct soars beneath the stars.

APPENDIX I

A SELECTION OF LETTERS

*by Lyonel Feininger to Alfred Vance Churchill
and H. Francis Kortheuer 1893–1913*

Twenty-four letters and postcards were written by Lyonel Feininger to Alfred Vance Churchill from May 20, 1890 to August 22, 1920; all are in the possession of the Archives of American Art, Detroit, Mich., and three of them are here reprinted. All references in the letters to Lyonel Feininger's personal and family affairs have been omitted.

The eighty-three letters and postcards sent by Feininger to H. Francis Kortheuer from August 20, 1884, to November 28, 1903, are in the possession of Mr. and Mrs. Dayrell Kortheuer of Charlotte, North Carolina; one of these has been reprinted here. Microfilms of these two sets of letters are kept by the Archives of American Art, Detroit, Mich. The four letters selected for inclusion in this study seemed most significant in relation to Feininger's development from cartoonist and illustrator to painter.

Since all of the Feininger letters available from the two sources mentioned above have been quoted from and commented on in the text, footnotes to them, as well as to the one letter written by Mr. H. Francis Kortheuer to the author, seemed unnecessary at this point. For information concerning the persons mentioned in these letters, the reader is asked to consult the index at the back of this book.

Lyonel Feininger to Alfred Vance Churchill, Berlin:

Berlin W. 62
Schill strasse 16 III
June 24th 1893.

My beloved Al!

Many thanks for your letter. When I read how great your love for me is, it almost terrifies me, for I often think I am most unworthy of it. Old man, you always were my good angel, and I need someone, oh! so badly! to open my be-cob-webbed heart to. I would value your presence here now more than earthly estimate. I am not in a hurry to go back to Paris, although my heart clings to it; for I have had sufficient preliminary studies to begin almost any practical illustrative work, and too long a delay impairs the *practical* worth of my study or its results. So I shall hire a small studio here in the Winter, and the comic papers shall be flooded with my drawings (this is a figure of speech).

Alfred old friend, Leo was the most austere, the sedatest student that (except yourself) ever went to Paris. Besides, on 80 marks a month, there is no great show for a rakish existence. My greatest sorrow was that I had at no one time enough money to study to my heart's-content. And I often went hungry to bed. It was invaluable to me to have made the experiment—I should have known no rest until I had convinced myself concerning french art. Now I am content to build up my own art for a while and as it is nowhere in all Europe easier than in Berlin to make a start, I am content to stay here yet a while. The majority of art-students are, as you say, *rotten*. Oh, I was disappointed in my countrymen. And the average frenchman flösst mir Abscheu ein. To say that this is a properly matured judgement, founded upon intimate knowledge of the french character would be foolish, and I came across traits in some of the most besmirched fellows that still showed the *race*, an inkling of inborn overcrusted nobility which did not as often strike my notice in americans. But the immorality is as *raffinirt* [sophisticated] and seems so much a matter of course throughout that it does and must repulse every man who believes in pure womanhood, and in something beyond the mere animal necessity for living. Old man, I can realize what a hard hard struggle it is for you to keep up a "Lust" for work, and what a longing and *absolute necessity* to see the work of other artists besides your own overpowers the best of determinations at times, and paralyzes ones efforts. I will look up some little note or sketch to send with this letter in the hope that it will bring some meaning with it which you can perceive and which will give you an idea or two for work.

With the object I have in view of working this Winter for the illustrated papers I spend one or two hours daily in making notes of all sorts of passers-by on the street, from our windows. And out of doors I do the same; also in restaurants etc. It is of the greatest value to me to acquire surety of hand and eye in this way —to seize instantly the character of an object whether animals or otherwise—and it is the surest method of gaining action to ones figures. What *Kopf-zer-brechen* [mental strain] hasn't it cost me to study the psychology of a woman's skirt in walking!

Alfred, old fellow, you ask me what I think of *realism* and *impressionism?* I will try to respond in very few words although were we together the subject is one which would be almost inexhaustable. Rembrandt and Titian had less to trouble them than the modern artist has. Their art found a more individual expression because Nature was purely the accessory object and the idea and its ideal expression only included the most necessary symbols of Nature, idealised or suppressed as the main idea demanded. Today, when every dabster has more advanced notions of true *reproduction of nature* than those old masters, it has become an imperative duty for every artist to keep in the march technically (by which I mean also ability to correctly see planes, tones, atmosphere etc) before he can with impunity *create*. Myself, I think this shows that in spite of improvements so called in art, the difficulties remain always the same. The race of artists may have comparatively no greater difficulty in keeping apace with the times technically but are no longer so easily and confidently able to keep from the danger of neglecting the *soul* of a picture in the attention given to the merely technical *outside*. Today, as centuries hence, the artist must *command* Nature, even when he gives her semblance the most accurately, and today the few great who can do so are as far above others as were the old Masters above *their* contemporaries. The only difference is that *mediocrity* is more brilliant to-day; indeed, in the past, mediocrity could not exist. I think there are practically the same conditions today as formerly, only in the rush to achieve the highest results in realistic painting after Nature pure and simple, the creation of *pictures* proper is left to the men of exceptional creative genius who really live in their ideas—and the rest are content to put forth studies, experiments, and motives void of all concreteness which they give some *titel* to and call pictures. The Salon is just a collection of studies. Every *picture* is doubly one by contrast. Al, old fellow, there the modern advance in seeing Nature correctly has produced a distinct set of artists which found its origin no doubt in the landscapist and includes the Still-life painter. (under the heading "still-life painter" comes the nude painter, the man who with a marvellous skill and understanding of the human form never could be a painter of any but studies). This latter is a very necessary class of artist, he keeps the standard of consumate *drawing* up, and drawing *is* the soul—of art tho' not *such* drawing. You would be surprised to hear how little *color* is regarded, provided it be accurate with Nature. Study *outline* Al! for figure. The french penwork is *superb*. So is L. L'Hermitte's charcoal work. I never saw an original *Monet*. I think that as far as a sculptor who merely rough-hews a statue, however splendid the blocked *proportions*, can be called *great*, so far can Monet be called the same.

Well, old chap, I will have to stop now. I shall not let too long a time elapse ere I again let you hear from me. I hope you will be able to make some use of the drawing of the barnyard I send. It is *not* ideal, and it is not, either, strictly drawn à la Hancke. You had better put it simply under glass with a white *mat* around, or else lay tissue paper over, as it rubs easily. I worked exclusively

50.   Feininger with bicycle.   1894.

on tone paper last year, but except in certain cases should hardly counsel its use. White is *truer*. Write soon. God bless you and your dear wife

Your faithful friend   Leo.

Lyonel Feininger to H. Francis Kortheuer, Friedenau bei Berlin:

Friedenau, [near Berlin]
Jan. 30th 1898
Albestrasse 16 I

My dear old Frank!

Your card of the 17th inst. came yesterday and made the day bright. . . .

You speak of old times, and they live fresh in my memory too! How short the days were when we used to be together; how *few*, too: I can recall it all so well! You generally had to leave me at 5–6 o'clock and oh, the pain of parting! When we think of it to-day, it seems hard to conceive that we should have been subject to Aunties and Papas in the matter of going home! I used to look forward to your visits a week before-hand, at the time you lived in Brooklyn in the Cumberland Ave, or in Flatbush at Mrs. — was it *Piersall?*

We were fanciful! and I doubt whether we changed a bit therein since! You are perhaps better protected against the detrimental effects of fancifulness by having a *positive* calling to follow—but I suffer yet under the laming influence of lively fancy. What does Teresa [Kortheuer's wife] think of us as boys? Hasn't she smiled over the old letters and the little trains? *Kindly*, of course! Do you think she will care to add a few lines in your letter as you say? It would give me great pleasure! I should value it! —And then—the days when I was in Plainfield—*why*, I often wonder, couldn't we have seen each other oftener? It used to be my one great pleasure to write to you and above all, to receive your letters in the jolly green, yellow, blue and pink envelopes I furnished for our correspondence! What an idea! to be sure! *There* showed the painter! (?) Why in Goodness name couldn't I have become a ship-builder or a locomotive manufacturer—even an engineer on an express train Never mind! it's better so as it is. . . .

We have had an unprecedented Winter this far. Since Jan 2nd not one day of frost, and today is no exception to the rule, for it is drizzling drearily. But several times we have had simply spring weather, and one night at 10 o'clock we had 48 2/10 Fahrenheit! I have covered over 400 miles in January on my wheel.

I shall have the satisfaction of putting away my *first 100* marks in the bank on Feb. 1st and shall add to it [at] every opportunity. It means *freedom* for me. Tell me which of the papers I send you interest you most—and if there are any among them you do *not* like or which you think *too loose* (I should send many more if I did not think always that they contained much that you would be repelled at) tell me so. The *"Narrenschiff"*, of which I sent the No. 1 is of the latter class, else I should have sent it regularly— but as they have come to me with a flattering invitation to contribute *"all I can, and every thing I wish"* I shall send such numbers in which my works appears. I do not believe the paper will have a long life—but the paint [of the color printing] is good and gives me a chance to do good work and everybody is trying to get in there, and few *can,* so that it is a good enough advertisement for me to be seen in it. I find that illustration is going through a remarkable stage again—many who *were* good and old-fashioned are trying to copy the new direction and are going right down, so that they begin to lose all standing by means of being open to the reproach of plagiarism and senseless mannerism. I myself admire much that is in the modern direction but am distinctly individual in my work, so that I am coming in demand as *modern* and yet as *original.* Others *copy* me much, tho' I could never pretend to be able to create followers in the strict sense. I crave after *serious* work and that is what I mean to turn to when I can properly study. The picture "Bürger Berlins, wahret Eure heiligsten Güter" ["Burgers of Berlin, safeguard your holiest possessions"] which I send you now has received praise and few accredited me with it, as it is not a caricature. It is not particularly good! but I enjoyed trying something else for a change. I have been off the hooks for several weeks, so have nothing I could care to send you.

I wonder what things will come to in Paris with the Dreyfuss Affair! They are on the verge of the greatest social calamity of the century—and it is a question not to be overlooked, as it may interfere with my plan of studying there next year, before coming to N.Y. if so, I should come direct to N. Y. . . .

I must "collapse" now, too! Write me a card now and then and it will answer the purpose if you are busy! To see your handwriting is a pleasure for me already.

Give my kindest regards to your dear aunt [Hilda Marshall] and [brother] Arthur and remember your old Leo to his rival, Teresa.

Your loving old friend

Feininger.

Lyonel Feininger to Alfred Vance Churchill, Zehlendorf bei Berlin:

Lyonel Feininger   Zehlendorf M.
                                    Koenigstr. 32
                                    Feb. 3rd, 1913.

Dear old Al!

God bless you, old fellow! your dear kind, generous words gave me the very greatest pleasure; no one would nor could write so but your dear self. As we get on in years (!) (I am, myself already 41! and Al must be about 52!) we learn ever the better that there is no new friendship can be so deep and enduring as the old, formed when we were young and could scarce imagine what golden, enduring ties we entered into, to bless our riper years. You met my old friend Kramer (I met him in the early 90s shortly after you left Germany, and it is about 19 years since I've seen *him*) in the Exhibit, and he wrote about it, and I asked him to give me your address, for it is many years since I've known where you are, But before his reply has arrived, comes your note!

That my work is a (shall we call it a "success"? or does it merely "attract attention")? "success" then!—is somewhat of a surprise to me; I responded to the invitation of the Photographische Gesellschaft to send over etchings, with considerable indifference —misgivings would not be the word—for I did not attach sufficient importance to my things to have any solicitude one way or the other about their ultimate acception. For, here in North Germany, there is little understanding for such and small encouragement extended to innovators, and I have long since learned to "keep dark, lie low and watch 'or rather,' *work*."

It is not given me, even if I so desired (which I do *not!*) to go the normal or beaten path in art—and it takes years and years of strenuous, unremitting and critical work & selfdisciplining to put forth a *new* form. And for my conviction, Art is ever *new*, being *Creation*. I am painting exclusively since about 3 years, although I keep up drawing for my own needs. But my work for the "papers" is at an end—there is no place for me there! The moment one goes one's own way, one is an outlaw. Thinking it would interest you, I will send some reproductions of my old cartoons, etc. They were adapted, under great difficulties, to the needs of pretty narrowminded and money-grabbing publishers, who would never understand a work of art for its own sake. Well, I had about 14 years of it, and never dreaming that there was for me such a thing in the world as *art,*—that was something quite outside of my treadmill existence. The awakening came like a wonder, to me. It is now some 5 years since I commenced to work for myself. I wish I could send you something to give you an idea, at least, of my line of development. I may have some latest pictures photo'ed, and then will send you copies. Above all, never, old Al, think me a "faddist"! I possessed the elements of so-called *cubism* before I had ever heard of such a thing or seen a cubistic painting—My work of 5 and more years ago shows already the tendancy towards a new and absolutely *personal perspective;* as to color—well, when I was but a mere hobbledehoy at the "Akademie" in '89, you called me a "colorist." Oh Al, dear old Al! if we could meet! Perhaps I may in a year or two come over to the States, after 26 years absence! My dear Father is living in New York. Well, you shall hear from me soon again! *Tell* me about yourself, how are you, and what work do you do? How I wish I could see your work! old friend! And your family? And I'll tell you about mine! I have 2 girls and three boys! They are wonderful children and I am very happy.

ever your old

Leo—

Lyonel Feininger to Alfred Vance Churchill, Zehlendorf-Mitte:

Zehlendorf-Mitte, March 13th 1913

Beloved old Al

You deserve better than "reproductions" from Leo; I have picked out a number of notes after Nature from 1909, '10, '11 and '12, made in the Summer at the Seaside (Heringsdorf on the Baltic, which is really *not* the Sea, but rather a great lake with brackish water, and Heringsdorf lies in one of the most enclosed corners of the Baltic) which will give you a very fair comparative standard of my late development. Having never painted before 1907, and for 15 years before that been merely a drudge at political cartoons for the bare necessities of sustenance for my family & self, (like yourself,) (but unlike yourself, with no hope nor real definite thought of ever becoming an artist!) it chanced that I never had fallen into Impressionism at all! My first pictures, after I commenced in oil, in April 1907, were caricatures in flat, decorative spots, after my *drawings* of such fantastic subject, made from time to time for my own relief. My vague ideal was, to approach to the style of certain crude signboards, just barely escaping "rankness," as understood among "*real*" painters. After a year, in 1908, I came to have the opportunity of drawing out of doors all Summer, and made very many notes, chiefly of figures, caricatured, and experimenting with *colored outlines* & contrasting surfaces. The few figure notes dated "1908" will show you these, and likewise, that I followed motions very closely. 1909 I first commenced to sketch landscape, still decorative, worshipful of Van Gogh. 1910 I had attained to greater rythm, somewhat neglecting color, of which I felt perfectly sure. 1911 my studies had brought me to the critical state where imitation of Nature is imminent, but in that Spring I had gone to Paris for 2 weeks and found the art-world there agog with cubism—a thing I had never heard even mentioned before, but which I had already, entirely intuitively, striven after *for years*. So my studies, after May 1911 (Paris) were, t'is true, impressionistic, but already *formulated,* more or less. & 1912 I worked entirely independantly, striving to wrest the secrets of atmospheric perspective & light & shade gradation, likewise rythm & balance between various objects, from Nature. My "cubism," to so miscall it, for it is the reverse of the french cubists aims, is based upon the principle of monumentality & *concentration* to the absolutest extreme possible, of my visions, either compositional or before Nature. The french, as far as I have followed the works of Picasso, Friesz, Delaunay & Le Fauconnier, *lose* the concentration of vision, and verge into chaotic dispersal of form & are actually reverting into a sort of neo-neo-impressionism.

My method, though it is not so much method, as *necessity,* or work, forbids me to reproduce an impression of Nature immediately in painting. I work after Nature to *learn,* and to collect and widen my knowledge—and my paintings show far more than my notes, what I have received from Nature. So, for the present, I cannot show you any reproduction of latest work, although I enclose a few photos of earlier work (lacking, of course, their greatest merit, *color.*) With each new picture I make giant strides, since the Fall [of] 1912; it seems to all accquainted or interested in my work, scarce credible—but I am building upon a foundation to endure, and am very sure, now, that I am following the only possible lines for my development.

Dear old friend! now you have the few explanations of my

sketches I am sending you, so that you can understand them best by comparing them. They are yours to keep, I have *thousands,* and can do without these.

How I did enjoy your dear letter, which came yesterday. 6 months ago I had one or two friends & enthusiasts—and was unknown to the public except as a former Witzblatt celebrity, really *quite* a celebrity of that cheapest of all renown, *publicity!* Now, since about 4 weeks, I am becoming an object of attention to the very most gifted of the younger striving artists & critics here. Our quiet domicile (except for 3 rampant boys!) is suddenly become the favorite meeting place for a number of young people (compared to my late maturing self, just like you, old Al!) and every week one or the other brings in a new Man who has become curious to know my work. It is gratifying but by no means upsetting to me, for I give not a "tinker's damn" for public approval, nor do I exhibit at all, this year, just *because* I am progressing.

Old friend Al! here I am talking "shop" and God knows how gladly I would talk about all that fills me, with you. Tell you about the *longing* that impels me to create, create, create! It is *only* that, not a thought for the others, what they think, say or care. Is not proof enough, that, up to last Winter in New York at The Photographische Gesellschaft's Exhibit, where you were, I have never yet sold a picture, etching or drawing? You have simply no idea what a crime originality is in Germany! With what distrust yea, insulting skepticism, the innovator is regarded & treated here. There is not even a "Père Tanguy" here, as for glorious unfortunate Van Gogh & the other martyrs!

How nobly you have held out, old friend! your life has been truly a hard struggle, and now that your prospects are brighter I am grateful & happy beyond words. I received your 3 photos and was very happy to see your pictures, full of luminosity & poetry, and quality, such as in Germany *none* possess. You do not realize, perhaps, the truth of this statement, but *German* impressionism is simply appalling! I wish I could see the *color* in your work. Your pictures *are* pictures. And what much struck me in your letter is the fact that we both, the more we ripen, realise the more that the *best* in us as *artists* was present in our childhood. I "hark back" since years, to my childish impressions; the monumentality, the freedom from conventional perspective trammeling the fantasy; all were strongest in the child, and it is surely for the ripening man to best realize them. So you are *surely* on the right path, if you have this longing to guide you. Either we are *born artists,* or else we can never become but imitators & Handwerker. The one thing you cannot *learn* is creativeness, originality! An Ober-lehrer can learn Impressionistic imitation; even a moderately gifted monkey, I should think!

Old Al, I cannot write now all I have to tell you; I won't even try, there is too much! I am anticipating getting off to dear little Weimar on Apl. 1st, where I intend to work out of doors, until October. This year is a critical one in my career, I expect to produce very important works. It is strange how, in the first year of my naive painting, 1908–9, I produced in a few months pictures which were far more valuable as creations than for 2 weary years later, during the period of intense study after Nature—and, as I mentioned before, a year of this time was a continual battling against Impressionism, due to said study; but those who say that we moderns have to go through the whole development, Impressionism and all, are perfectly right! It *may* be spared our descendants. But now I am triumphant over it and can all the more hope to realise my inner visions. You write, with golden humor, of yourself that you are "Kiddish"! I am the same as you, far younger with 41¾ years than all the 25 & 30 year old artists I am acquainted with, but likewise, far less hampered with Schul-Weisheit.

Soon I will send you a few reproductions out of my former days, cartoons & such like. It often astonishes me to see how much my work, strained as it was & perverted to suit the brutes I was dependant on for my living, showed of what now is developing into being, artistically, I was invariably rated & *threatened with loss of position* for the very traits which make me an artist of original power! And today I should actually have to go begging or else turn to woodchopping or selling cheese or some such useful occupation, if dependant on those "brutes." Thank God that it is *not* necessary. Al, when not working, (which is always) and when working mentally "only," I play Bach & Buxtehude on my Estey Harmonium; music is as much my life as air and creating in paint. My pictures are ever wearing closer the Synthesis of the fugue; not one unnecessary spot, or which will not bear analysis with reference to the whole. That is my *formal* aim. Have you thought over this *primal* element of *enduring* art? Cubism *is* a synthesis, but may easily be degraded into mechanism. I had the courage to start out absolutely mechanically to work through to the *living* form; my "cubism" (again, falsely so-called, call it rather, if it *must* have a name, "prismism," although that is but one element of it) is *visionary,* not physical.

But now enough for today, good bye & God bless you, old friend! I was even happy to know that you are 3 or 4 years younger than I believed! And a Kid yet, Salah!

Your old, faithful

Leo.

Give my love to Marie and your boy!

Julia returns your kind greetings, and my mother, who has just dropped in & is reading your letter, tells me she holds you still in kindest remembrance!

P.S. Don't fear that I shall, or my art, rather, escape you, if I can help it!

Leo

APPENDIX II

Letter of H. Francis Kortheuer, Daytona Beach, Florida, to
Dr. Ernst Scheyer, Detroit, Mich.:

H. Francis Kortheuer
709 Goodall Avenue
Daytona Beach
Florida

March 18th [19]59

Dear Dr. Scheyer

In your letter of Feb. 27th you asked for a short biographical sketch of my life, with stress on my relation with Leo.

As you know, Carl Feininger, Leo's father, was a violinist— My father—Hermann O. C. Kortheuer was a concert pianist, composer and lecturer on theory of music.

Both being musicians, they naturally became acquainted— probably in New York. That was some time before my father married.

I was born June 12, 1873 in Bergen on the heights, now a part of Jersey City, New Jersey.

My mother, born Florence Mary Marshall died in 1878 leaving my younger brother Arthur and me.

My father took us to Ohio and left us there with his relatives.

Later we were brought back to New York City to live with my mother's family among which was my grandmother and aunt Hilda Marshall.

We lived in an apartment at No. 429 West 57th street, New York City.

The Feininger family, Mr. & Mrs. Carl Feininger, Leo, Helen and Elsa lived across the street in No. 430.

Leo and I soon became acquainted and intimate as we had similar interests.

My aunt Hilda, an amateur artist, seeing that we both liked to draw, used to give us lessons in drawing from still life.

I believe that was Leo's first instruction in drawing.

At that time Leo was being taught violin by his father, and sometimes when I went over across the street I would find him busy practicing and not permitted to come and draw pictures with me.

Leo and I always spoke English together although he probably knew some German; Helen and Elsa knew little then.

On the contrary, my father never spoke English with me until I was 10 or 11 years old. My mother & her family did not know German.

My early schooling was in two private schools where German was spoken & I also had some Latin.

Later I went to public school, Grammar School No. 69 on 54th St, graduated from there & went to College of the City of New York Class of/95 but did not graduate there—also night school at Cooper Union N. Y.

Leo also went to grammar school 69 but not at the same time I was there, for, being two years older he probably left school after two years to go to work.

He worked in Wall Street as a messenger probably in a brokers office.

That was after Mrs. Feininger with Helen and Elsa left for Germany, and Leo lived in a boarding house in Plainfield New Jersey (about 25 miles from New York)

I remember going out there to visit him and staying overnight.

The woman who kept the boarding house must have been a disagreeable person for she wrote (or told) Mr. Feininger that Leo spent so much time writing to me and drawing pictures of the Jersey Central R. R. trains when he should be "better employed."

Leo had a lot of little varicolored envelopes addressed to me —(you may find some among the letters to me.)

I do not think that Mr. Feininger took her complaint very seriously because Leo told me later that his father seeing, but not reading, the colored envelopes said jokingly "what are these? easter eggs?"

The books we read as small boys included Jules Verne's stories "Around the World in 80 days"—Fenimore Cooper's sea stories—also some of Dickens.

Leo apparently at that time was not interested in the classics, like the Iliad & Odyssey—which I read in translations, having only "small Latin," and no Greek.

As I see it now—it was probably that Leo never came across these books.

We did not play baseball like most boys or indulge in outdoor sports—All I remember is going on picnics in Central Park.

For our amusement we used to draw what we called Concert pieces—they were scrawls attempting to caricature orchestras showing the violinists with their instruments held upside down etc.

We both liked locomotives and boats. There is a small pond in Central Park near 72nd St. & 5th Ave. which is arranged with facilities for sailing model yachts.

There Leo used to sail a beautifully made little yacht which he made. I carved out a hull about two feet long for a boat I fitted out with a motor and batteries to have it electrically propelled.

We whittled out little model locomotives and cars and painted them to show the wheels, windows, and names of the railroads. These are quite small, about 3 inches long, & I still have a few of them.

As little boys we had our fantasies which we kept secret from the adults, feeling that they would not approve of such dreamy nonsense.

In our imagination we pictured ourselves as kings or rulers of our realms.

Leo was king of his country—called it Colonora and he drew maps of his country, plans of a city showing and naming the streets with tram car lines etc. He also drew pictures of his ships and steamboats & men-of-war to fight the pirates!

I did the same thing and called my country Columbia.

Later Mr. Feininger moved to 4th Ave. Going over to see them I found Leo and Elsa playing a game on the dining room table. It was supposed to be a seafight between their respective ships.

They were bombarding one another's ships (made of cigar boxes) with checkers snapped across by bending table knives.

Leo called out as I came "I am beating Elsa."

Another time when the Feiningers were living over on the west side of the city, 15th or 16th street—Leo & I went over and stood on the sidewalk on 8th Avenue to see Barnum's Circus parade—

We had tin blowpipes and blew dried peas at the animals and acrobats as they passed.

As a small boy I doubt if Leo had any definite idea of becoming an artist.

He liked to draw and paint and make little model locomotives —but so did I.

He did play the violin and may have thought that was his future.

My business life work was development engineering, specializing in telephony. For 36 years I was with the Western Electric Co. & then the Bell Telephone Laboratories—I retired in 1933.

When Leo came back to America in 1936 it was 50 years since we had seen one another. So I figure that he left here in 1886. The letters you have which he wrote to me will confirm that, I believe.

Sometime after Leo's departure from here, Frederick Strothmann was introduced to me; I think it was by a letter from Leo.

Strothmann, who lived in Staten Island, used at that time to go to Berlin to study painting at the Academy. While there he became well acquainted with Leo and his family. Mrs. Karl Feininger called him "Fritz." And we used to call him that for the rest of his life.

Fritz told anecdotes about his association with Leo abroad.

They had a room together—perhaps did some painting there. Some paint marks got on the window curtains and to hide them they painted them over with white paint.

It appears that they also lived together for a time studying in Paris.

Fritz told us about Leo's unexpected skill in ice skating and his prowess in bicycle riding.

Fritz and Leo were in love with the same girl. Leo married her and had two daughters who are still living I was told.

It is unfortunate that Fritz became so ill that he was in no condition to be interviewed. For various reasons I did not see him during the last 2 years or so of his life. He was a good friend to us all for the rest of his life.

He died in May 1958.

Had he lived he could have contributed things of interest concerning Leo's artistic development.

Leo's liking for boats and trains came out later when he made model yachts, which I understand he sailed with his boys on the Baltic.

He also made wooden toy railroad trains.

A few years ago, Leo when talking to me remarked that there were four of us that he associated together—first, the artist Kramer, much older than the rest and not living for some time, next Leo himself, then Fritz and last, myself. Then he said "You are the baby."

So he associated three artists and one technical man.

I felt quite flattered to be included, but after all my work also called for creative imagination, which he recognized.

Since Leo came back—for the most time, we, that is my wife and family, and Leo & Julia have been much together—They used to rent a summer cottage two miles from us in Connecticut (Falls Village) and also we used to visit them at Stockbridge, Mass. and in New York City.

To write this letter longhand has been an effort—it has been done by installment, which accounts for the delay in answering yours—

Finally I can tell you that Leo as a boy was the same gentle lovable character that he was as a man—

Cordially yours
Frank Kortheuer

NOTES

Chapter I

1. This spelling of the name "Lyonel" is used throughout this study. In letters and in signatures during the earlier years the name is often spelled Léonell or Lyonell, with occasional abbreviations into Leo. According to H. F. Kortheuer, Feininger was christened Léonell but changed this spelling to Lyonel after he had come to Germany. The etchings of 1911 are signed with a witty inversion of letters: Leinoel Einfinger (Linseedoil Onefinger).

2. A water color by Churchill, *Friedrichstrasse in Rain,* done circa 1890 and now in the Scrapbook kept by him, could easily be mistaken for a work by the early Feininger if it were not for Churchill's full signature in the bottom corner.

3. Churchill has written the story of Oberlin College since its foundation, including that of his family, in a series of articles under the title "Midwestern" which appeared during several years in the *Northwest Ohio Quarterly,* starting in XXIII, No. 1 (no dates available). The College, though outstanding in music from the beginning offered during these early years nothing in the field of the visual arts. Churchill, the son of an outstanding musician, had enjoyed an excellent training in music while he studied at the Conservatory connected with Oberlin College, but had never seen an important original painting before he "left home at the age of twenty-three," as he stated in his "Midwestern" reminiscences.

4. Among Churchill's American teaching positions were: Iowa College (now Grinnell College), 1891–93; St. Louis (Missouri) 1893–97; the headship of the Art Department of Teachers College, Columbia University, New York, 1897–1905. Churchill held lectureships at Johns Hopkins University, Baltimore, Maryland, in 1902, and at the University of Chicago in 1914, 1916, and 1917 and was generally in wide demand for single lectures at American colleges and museums, among them the Detroit Institute of Arts.

5. Henry-Russell Hitchcock, "Alfred Vance Churchill's Activity at the Smith College Museum." Seventy-fifth Anniversary of Smith College, Northampton, Mass. 1946. Churchill's chief artistic interests during his years at Smith were Géricault, Corot and, generally, French landscape painting in the nineteenth and early twentieth centuries.

Chapter II

1. Lyonel Feininger died on January 13, 1956, at 235 East 22nd Street, not far from the house of his birth. His widow is still living in the East 22nd Street apartment.

2. The staff of the New York College of Music (founded in 1876) were exclusively either born or trained in Germany. The *Männergesangsverein* (Oratorium Society), founded in 1874 by Leopold Damrosch, and the New York Symphony Society, also founded by Damrosch four years later and continued after his death by his son Walter, are further examples.

3. Charlotte Teller, "Feininger—Fantasist." *The International Studio,* LXIII, No. 249 (Nov. 1917).

4. *Annals of the New York Stage,* edited by C. D. Odell, vols. 8–12. Columbia University Press. (n. d.)

5. *Lyonel Feininger, Exhibition,* July–August 1941, Detroit, Institute of Arts—the Russell A. Alger House, Grosse Pointe Branch. Preface by Perry T. Rathbone.

6. Alfred H. Barr, *Lyonel Feininger—Marsden Hartley,* New York: 1944, p. 8. Hereafter quoted as "Barr."

7. Barr, p. 8.

8. "Feininger and Sons," *Life,* XXXI, No. 20 (Nov. 12, 1951).

9. Woodcut of such "Draisinenfahrer" after W. P. Snyder in *Harper's Weekly,* 1879.

10. Reprod. Willy Wolfradt, "Lyonel Feininger," *Jahrbuch für Junge Kunst,* 1924, p. 63. The oil representing the same subject, "Velocipedists," is of 1910 (Oeuvre Cat. No. 50).

11. Lothar Schreyer, *Lyonel Feininger: Dokumente und Visionen,* München: 1957.

12. Barr, p. 8.

13. Harry T. Peters, *Currier & Ives: Printmakers to the American People,* New York: 1942, p. 20. One of the best artists employed by the firm was Louis Maurer (born in Bieberich-on-the-Rhine, 1832). Since he was also an accomplished musician, Lyonel Feininger's father might have known him.

14. T. Lux Feininger, "Two Painters," *Chrysalis,* Boston: IX, No. 9–10, 1956.

15. Hans Hess, *Lyonel Feininger,* Stuttgart: W. Kohlhammer Verlag, 1959. Reprod. p. 1, IX, lower row, right. Hereafter quoted as "Hess."

16. Kortheuer Letters, Plainfield, New Jersey, August 25, 1887, and Sept. 10, 1887.

17. Hess, *op. cit.,* p. 7.

18. Barr, p. 8.

19. Alexander Liberman, "Feininger," *Vogue,* CXXVII (April 15, 1956), p. 90–95.

20. Oeuvre Cat. No. 157. The oil is dated 1916, once in the coll. of Walter Rathenau, now in the artist's estate.

21. Alexander Liberman, *op. cit.*

22. Frederic S. Wight, "Feininger in Lincoln," catalog Preface to *The Work of Lyonel Feininger,* Cleveland Museum of Art, 1951, p. 11.

23. Barr, p. 11.

24. Mrs. Julia Feininger writes about this theater in a letter to the author:
    We once created a theatre, doing everything [ourselves], Leo the scenery—adorable, perfectly charming—and phantastic underwater

scenes, woods in moonlight, etc.—I did the "actors" on strings and the text; a friend of ours [did] the electrical lighting apparatus—it was a combined family achievement.

25. Charlotte Teller, *op. cit.*
26. Reprod. Hess, p. 5.

Chapter III

1. Kortheuer Letters, Berlin, December 20, 1897.
2. Frederic Wight, *op. cit.*, p. 11.
3. Ernst Barlach, *Ein Selbsterzähltes Leben*. First ed. Berlin: 1921.
4. Kortheuer Letters, Hamburg, February 27, 1888.
5. Kortheuer Letters, July, 29, 1888.
6. Kortheuer Letters, Berlin 7. September 1888.
7. William A. Murrell, *History of American Graphic Humor*, New York: 1938, p. 93.
8. An "Extrait de la Gazette de Liège du 23 septembre 1890" included in the Feininger-Churchill papers shows that the college had all the departments of a University.
9. Hess, *op. cit.*, p. 8.
10. Especially those in the letter to Churchill of October 7, 1890: *Feininger learning the French A B C's; Feininger made fun of by the boys; Feininger playing with a hoop* and its result: Feininger fallen to the ground, the hoop spinning around one of his long legs.
11. *Jesuits I* of 1908 (Oeuvre Cat. No. 27), *Jesuits II* of 1913 (Oeuvre Cat. No. 114), *Jesuits III* of 1915 (Oeuvre Cat. No. 135).
12. Collège St. Servais, Liège, November 16, 1890 and November 24, 1890.
13. Joseph Pennell, born 1858 in Philadelphia, active in London, died in New York 1926. Wrote *Pen Drawing* and *Pen Draughtsmen*.
14. Edwin Austin Abbey, born 1852 in Philadelphia, died 1911. Studied at the Philadelphia Art Academy. After 1871 he was among the chief illustrators of *Harper's Magazine*. After 1883 he lived in England and "recreated in his sensitive line drawings over the years the small Tudor villages, the odd rustic characters" (Larkin, Oliver W., *Art and Life in America*, New York: 1949, and *E. A. Abbey* by E. V. Lucas, New York: 1921, 2 vols.). He became best known through his illustrations for Shakespeare and his frieze in the Boston Public Library. Originally a graphic artist, he turned later to watercolor and oils of historical subjects.
15. Barr, p. 12.
16. Reprod. Charlotte Teller, *op. cit.*, p. 27.
17. Reprod. Hess, p. 17.
18. Ernst Hancke, born October 9, 1834 in Berlin; since 1857 pupil of the Berlin Academy, taught first at the Berlin *Kunst—und Gewerbeschule*, later at the Royal Art Academy there until 1912. He died in Berlin in 1914. His fields were portrait, history and genre painting.
19. Adolf Schlabitz, born 1854, had studied at the Berlin Academy from

1875 to 1882. He spent some time later at the Academie Julian in Paris and was thus quite well equipped for his job as art tutor.

20. Compare the drawing reprod. in Hess, p. 8.

21. Woldemar Friedrich, born 1846 in Gnadau (Province Sachsen), died 1910 in Berlin. Pupil of Steffeck in Berlin until 1865, then became a Professor at the Royal Art Academy, Berlin, in 1885. He studied later with Ramberg at the Weimar *Kunstschule,* where he became a teacher in 1887. As a result of his stay in Weimar, he published seventeen drawings for Goethe's *Life.* His numerous frescoes in public buildings are characteristic of the work of an established academician in Imperial Germany. At the time that Feininger was his pupil, he did the "Wandmalereien" at the *Buchhändler-börse* in Leipzig (1891–92) and those in the "Aula of the Gymnasium in the Luthertown Wittenberg." He was also a prolific illustrator for "Family" journals and could easily procure commissions for his gifted student Feininger.

22. Fred Werner, born 1869 in Australia, studied organ in Berlin with Franz Gruenicke; lived in Lindfield, N.S.W. Australia. For a while, Werner shared rooms with Feininger in Berlin.

23. The first Fugue was composed 1921; twelve other fugues followed. *Fuge VI fuer Orgel oder Klavier zu drei Händen* was composed in 1922 and the only one among the thirteen published (in *Europa Almanach,* 1925).

24. Reprod. Hess, p. 14, 15.

25. Jules Verne (1828–1905) was one of the first writers to exploit the possibilities of science as material for adventure tales. His books were regularly illustrated with wood engravings by Riou. Even the newer editions in the Librarie Hachette, Paris, are still published with these illustrations. Though often awkward, especially in figures, they are done in a dramatic chiaroscuro, influenced by Doré, which appealed to Feininger. Edouard Riou (1833–1900), Paris, was chiefly active as a wood engraver-illustrator for the Magazine "Le Tour du Monde" and of the books of Jules Verne and Walter Scott (since 1863).

26. Feininger also worked for another Harper publication *Harper's Round Table.* In the May 7, 1895, issue were "four little sketches. . . . Sister Sue's dream about Brother Tommy" (Letter to Kortheuer from Berlin, May 18, 1895).

27. See also the three photos of Feininger dedicated to Churchill, dated June 1894, in the Archives of American Art, Detroit.

28. Adolf Oberländer, born 1845 in Regensburg and the son of an organist, started his artistic career in Munich at the age of 16. Since 1862 pupil of Piloty at Munich Academy. Active also as painter. He gained fame, chiefly as caricaturist for *Fliegende Blätter,* for which he was active since 1863. He died in Munich in 1923, the greatest German cartoon humorist since W. Busch.

29. A. B. Frost; see Murrell, *op. cit.,* p. 36, 39, 70, 74, 100, 111.

30. Frederick Burr Opper; see Murrell, *op. cit.,* p. 26, 27, 57, 89, 103, 111, 113, 130, 132, 134, 135, 140, 175, 177.

31. Reprod. in Murrell, *op. cit.,* p. 75.

32. Murrell, *op. cit.,* p. 116.

33. Letter to Kortheuer, December 1894.

34. Quoted by Hess, p. 25.

35. T. L. Feininger, "Two Painters," *op. cit.*, p. 9/10.

36. Walter Mehring, *Verrufene Malerei*, Zürich, 1958, p. 78.

37. Reprod. Walter Mehring, *op. cit.*, p. 80, opposite a cartoon by Juan Gris for *L'Assiette au Beurre*, Paris 1910, which shows a stylistic relationship to Feininger's caricatures for *Le Témoin*.

38. Reprod. *Lyonel Feininger, Karikaturen 1898–1910*, Katalog No. 20. Published in Germany by the Dept. of Cultural Affairs, American Embassy.

39. An especially biting attack against the exclusive dueling fraternities is reproduced in Walter Mehring, *op. cit.*, p. 82: a student and a bum lie drunk on the pavement. The caption reads: "A privileged one."

40. Preface to the catalog of Feininger exhibition held in Munich, October 1954, organized by the *Bayerische Akademie der Schönen Künste*.

41. Professor Arthur Berson, metereologist and balloonist, was born Aug. 6, 1859 in Neusandez, Poland, and died in Berlin on Jan. 10, 1943. He had made approximately one hundred scientific balloon ascents between 1891 and 1911. He held (together with Reinhard Suering) the world record of 10,800 metres in 1901, a record not surpassed until 1916 (See biography and bibliography by R. Suering, *Zeitschrift fuer Technische Physik*, X, 1929). Feininger occasionally used the envelopes of the *Redaktion der Zeitschrift fuer Luftschiffahrt*. He was often a visitor to the offices of this magazine at the *Schinkel Platz* in Berlin. Berson was also the owner of some of Feininger's earliest paintings.

42. *Lyonel Feininger: Karikaturen 1898–1910, op. cit.*, fig. 125.

43. Reprod., Catalogue Lyonel Feininger Gedächtnis Ausstellung 1871–1956, No. 64, Museums Hamburg, Essen, Baden-Baden: 1961. The original design in pen, charcoal and watercolor, signed "Feininger" in the possession of Dr. Bernhard Sprengel, Hannover.

44. Reproduced H. Hess, *op. cit.*, p. 21. The cartoon appeared in *Lustige Blätter*, No. 27, Berlin: 1907. (From the collection Beilhack, Munich.)

45. A cartoon in the possession of the Galerie Alex Vömel, Düsseldorf (Exhibited, *Lyonel Feininger, Gedächtnisausstellung*, Cat. No. 63, 1961), is entitled *Germania in China*. It satirizes the political aspirations of Germany in the Far East.

46. Reprod. Hess, p. 18.

47. *Lyonel Feininger, Karikaturen 1898–1910; op. cit.*, Preface by Joachim Wachtel.

48. *Ibid.*, fig. 66, 96.

49. *Ibid.*, fig. 90.

50. *Ibid.*, fig. 107, 108, 140.

51. *Ibid.*, fig. 114.

52. Kortheuer Letters, June 15, 1896.

53. April 10, 1897.

54. December 20, 1897.

55. Georg Hermann, *Die Deutsche Karikatur im Neunzehnten Jahrhundert,* Bielefeld und Leipzig, 1901, p. 127. Hermann was probably the

most effective popularizer of the "Biedermeier-Revival." His novels *Jettchen Gebert* (1906) and *Henriette Jacoby* (1908), were both set during the Jewish Biedermeier milieu of Berlin and Potsdam. These novels were a sensational success in Germany, though not so lasting as Thomas Mann's *Buddenbrooks,* published earlier in 1901 and also depicting the same period. Hermann's introductory essay to *Das Biedermeier im Spiegel seiner Zeit* (Published by Deutsches Verlagshaus Bong & Co., Berlin-Leipzig-Wien-Stuttgart, 1913), is a fine analysis of this period. A recent evaluation of this period is in Ernst Scheyer, *Biedermeier in der Literatur und Kunstgeschichte,* Kulturwerk Schlesien, Würzburg: 1960.

56. Berlin National Galerie, *Austellung zum 60, Geburtstag von Lyonel Feininger, 1931,* Vorwort von Ludwig Thormaehlen.

57. Eugen Roth, *Simplicissimus,* Hannover: 1954, p. 88.

58. Bruno Paul (born 1874), later one of Germany's important architects. Concerning him, see: F. Ahlers-Hestermann, *Bruno Paul oder die Wucht des Komischen,* Berlin: 1960.

59. H. Hess, p. 20.

60. Georg Hermann, *op. cit.,* p. 127.

61. Reprod. H. Hess, p. 17.

62. Reprod., Georg Hermann, *op. cit.,* p. 122. Originally published in *Narrenrad.*

63. Reprod. Hermann, *loc. cit.*

64. Reprod. Barr, p. 15.

65. Reprod. Georg Hermann, *op. cit.,* p. 123.

66. Ernst Scheyer, *op. cit.,* p. 8.

67. Eugen Roth, *op. cit.,* p. 84–87.

68. G. Hermann, *op. cit.,* p. 113.

69. Reprod. Hess, p. 17.

70. Oeuvre Cat. No. 246.

71. Approximately half a century later Yale University commissioned Feininger to design the ex-libris for the "Thomas Mann Collection of Books and Papers."

72. On the occasion of sending Churchill two photos of himself on a bicycle, Feininger writes on October 8, 1897, "the wheel, the latest Cleveland back racer year 88 . . . I ride the trifle of 6–700 miles a month." The Kortheuer letters also speak at great length of his "passion for the wheel."

73. Wassily Kandinsky painted *Crinolines* twice in 1909, the first done in eighteenth-century Rococo style, the second in nineteenth-century Biedermeier style. Reprod. W. Grohmann, *Wassily Kandinsky,* New York, 1958, p. 351, No. 30. Original in S. R. Guggenheim Mus., New York, No. 89.

74. W. Wolfradt, *Jahrbuch der Jungen Kunst,* Leipzig: 1920, p. 64.

75. The exhibition referred to as *Deutsche Jahrhundert Ausstellung* owes much to the initiative of Julius Meier-Graefe. Its organiser was the Museum's Director, Hugo von Tschudi, who also wrote the introduction to the catalog. Reprinted in H. V. Tschudi, *Gesammelte Schriften zur Neueren Kunst,* München: 1912.

76. Barr, p. 11.

77. According to the "Questionaire" which Feininger answered on the occasion of the show in the Museum of Modern Art, New York, and preserved there in the library.

Chapter IV

1. Quoted in Eberhard Ruhmer, *Lyonel Feininger*, Munich: 1961, p. 10.
2. Peter Selz, *German Expressionist Painting*, Univ. of Calif., 1957, p. 278.
3. A copy of the letter was sent to the author by Mrs. M. Moll. See also Ernst Scheyer, *Die Kunst Akademie Breslau und Oskar Moll*, Würzburg: 1961, p. 56–57.
4. Margarete Moll, "Erinnerungen an Henri Matisse," *Neue Deutsche Hefte*, No. 23, Feb. 1956.
5. *Les Tendances nouvelles*, No. 56, circa 1912, p. 1338–40. Quoted after H. Hess, bibliography I: G1a.
6. The poem appeared in full in the magazine *Der Querschnitt*.
7. P. Selz, *op. cit.*, p. 278.
8. Reprod. in color, Hess, p. 49.
9. Friedrich Ahlers-Hestermann, *Pause vor dem dritten Akt*, Hamburg: 1949, p. 114. The author also wrote a magazine article on the subject of the Café: "Der deutsche Küntstlerkreis des Café du Dôme in Paris," in *Kunst und Künstler*, Berlin, XVI, 1917–18.
10. Hans Purrmann, *Ausstellung Württembergischer Kunstverein*, Stuttgart, September 1950. Preface to the catalog.
11. Gertrude Stein, *The Autobiography of Alice B. Toklas*, New York: 1933, p. 121.
12. Alfred Werner, *Jules Pascin*, New York: 1963.
13. *Ibid.*, p. 19, fig. 8.
14. Reprod. Hess, p. 43.
15. Reprod. Hess, p. 33.
16. Reprod. Hess, p. 39.
17. Reprod. Hess, p. 42.
18. Friedrich Ahlers-Hestermann, *op. cit.*, p. 131, 137.
19. Hess, p. 34–35.
20. Hess, p. 36.
21. Oeuvre Cat. No. 227.
22. Eberhard Ruhmer, *op. cit.*, p. 13.
23. Oeuvre Cat. No. 188.
24. *Le Témoin* drawing reprod. Barr, p. 15. Painted version reprod. Hess, p. 173, Oeuvre Cat. No. 23.
25. J. Thrall Soby, *Juan Gris*, New York: 1958, p. 13.
26. J. Thrall Soby, *op. cit.*, reprod., p. 13. The original drawing done in ink, pencil and gouache is in the coll. of Mr. and Mrs. B. J. Reis, New York. Other cartoons by Juan Gris are reprod. p. 12 and p. 120. The subject of J. Gris as cartoonist is more fully dealt with in D. H. Kahnweiler, *Juan Gris, Sa Vie, Son oeuvre, Ses écrits*, Paris: 1946.

27. Ernst Scheyer, "Far Eastern Art and French Impressionism," *Art Quarterly*, Detroit, Spring 1943, p. 140, footnote 3, also Ernst Scheyer, "Japonism," *Encyclopedia of the Arts*, New York, 1946, p. 509–511.

28. Ashbjornson, P., and Moe, J. (eds.) *Norwegische Volksmärchen für die Jugend bearbeitet*, introduction by Hermann Bang, sixteen illustrations by Lyonel Feininger. Includes preface by Ludwig Tieck originally written in 1846. Berlin: H. Bondy, 1908.

29. Philip Hofer, *The Artist and the Book 1860–1960*, Boston: 1961, p. 79.

30. Barr, p. 11.

31. Photo in the Library of the Museum of Modern Art, New York.

32. Hess, p. 24.

33. *Ibid.*, p. 101–2.

34. Wilhelm Busch, *Max and Moritz*, edited and annotated by H. Arthur Klein, trans. H. A. Klein and others. New York: Dover, 1962, p. 206 fn.

35. Aline Louchheim, "Feininger Looks Back on Eighty Years," *New York Times*, March 23, 1952.

36. *Lyonel Feininger, Exhibit, Detroit Institute of Arts—The Russell Alger House, Grosse Pointe, July–August 1941*. Preface by P. T. Rathbone. Excerpts from Letters 1905–1914. Both letters quoted on p. 98 are from this collection.

37. Hess, p. 43.

38. Barr, p. 11.

39. Previous exhibitions of drawings and etchings by Lyonel Feininger in Berlin: Eighth Exhibition of Berlin's Secession, 1903, and *Grosse Kunstausstellung*, 1904.

40. Postcard, Berlin, Pschorr Brewery, Oct. 22, 1894, a so-called "Bier Karte."

41. Feininger is in error. Churchill was then forty-eight years old.

42. Oeuvre Cat. No. 48.

43. The Detroit Institute of Arts. It is the first oil by Feininger purchased by an American public collection (1921)—through the Director, Dr. W. R. Valentiner.

44. T. L. Feininger, "Two Painters," *op. cit.*

45. Richard Goetz, painter, art dealer and famous wit. Concerning him, see: F. Ahlers-Hestermann, *Pause vor dem dritten Akt*, p. 135. Feininger mentions in a letter to Julia, Paris, May 12, 1911, that Goetz accompanied him on a trip to Meudon to look at "the magnificent viaducts."

46. *Lyonel Feininger, Gedächtnisausstellung.* Preface to the catalog by Alfred Hentzen. Includes excerpts of letters to Julia 1905–1931. Pub. 1961.

47. *Société des Artistes Indépendants*, La 27me Exposition, April / June 1911.

48. Charlotte Teller, *op. cit.*

49. Oeuvre Cat. No. 79. A *Still Life* of 1909, Oeuvre Cat. No. 38, also shows the influence of Matisse.

50. Oeuvre Cat. No. 137. Another such painting is the *Self Portrait with Clay Pipe* of 1910, Oeuvre Cat. No. 55, which is flat and decorative, but not yet cubist.

51. P. Selz, *op. cit.,* p. 279.

52. W. Grohmann, *Karl Schmidt-Rottluff,* Stuttgart: 1956. Reprod., p. 195.

53. H. Walden organised exhibits of works by Feininger in June 1916 together with Felix Mueller (42nd *Sturm* Exhib.) and a One-Man Show in Sept. 1917 (55th *Sturm* Exhib.).

54. L. Schreyer, *Dokumente und Visionen, op. cit.,* p. 7.

55. Theodor Däubler, "Lyonel Feininger," *Das junge Deutschland,* No. 10, Berlin: 1919.

56. Feininger sent Churchill another important article concerning his work. It was written by A. Schardt and published in *Das Kunstblatt,* edited by Paul Westheim, vol 6, 1922, No. 3. A. Schardt, later Professor of Art History at Immaculate Heart College, Los Angeles, USA, met Feininger again in 1954 in Stockbridge, Massachusetts.

57. "Lyonel Feininger Woodcut Artist" in *American Art Student,* p. 18, Jan. 1924. A pencil drawing by Feininger entitled "Environs of Paris" (1911) was purchased in the same year by the Smith College Museum through its Director at that time, Alfred Churchill. According to information obtained from the present Director the drawing is no longer in the possession of the Smith College Museum. An exchange of letters between Galka Scheyer (October 25, 1924) and Mr. Churchill (October 29, 1924) mentions that "a small picture" by Lyonel Feininger was purchased at that time either by the Smith College Museum or by Mr. Churchill for his own collection.

58. Letter quoted in the article, but not among the collection of Letters in the Archives of American Art, Detroit.

59. Lothar Schreyer, *Erinnerungen an Sturm und Bauhaus,* Munich 1956, p. 131.

60. Knoblauch dedicated his *Dada* (published by K. Wolff, Leipzig 1919) in the series *Der Jüngste Tag* to Feininger. The dedication reads: "Leo Feininger waffenbrüderlich zugeeignet." (Dedicated to Leo Feininger, brother-in-arms.) The small volume is decorated with an untitled woodcut by Leo Feininger: on a black background, white "little people" with stove-pipe hats are standing under a radiating star in a style characteristic of Feininger's mixture of the mysterious and the humorous.

61. Correspondence between Feininger and Knoblauch published by L. Schreyer in *Leo Feininger Dokumente und Visionen,* Langen-Mueller Verlag, Muenchen: 1957. See further: L. Schreyer, *Erinnerungen an Sturm & Bauhaus,* Munich: 1956, p. 155–56.

62. Lyonel Feininger, a member of the politically progressive artists and writers who made up the "November-Gruppe," certainly sympathized with the overthrow of the Kaiser and the establishment of a democratic republic. He was among the contributors to a pamphlet *An alle Künstler* (Berlin 1919) though only with a woodcut. Among the other contributors were: J. R. Becher, Walter Hasenclever, Kurt Eisner, Paul Zech, Max Pechstein, and Ludwig Meidner.

63. Hess, p. 45.

64. Hess, p. 175.

Chapter V

1. *The Work of Lyonel Feininger,* Catalog. Cleveland Museum of Art, 1951, No. 235.
2. Hess, p. 56.
3. The Work of Lyonel Feininger, Cleveland Museum of Art, 1951. Catalog: reprod. Plate XVII, No. 155, F 1884. According to Leona F. Prasse, who compiled this part of the catalogue, the numbers preceded by "F" are the artist's key numbers.
4. H. Hess, *Dank in Farben: Aus dem Gästebuch Alfred und Thekla Hess,* München: 1957.
5. H. Hess, *op. cit.,* p. 94–95. A conscious use of the manner of a child's drawing may be found in the watercolor *On the pier (An dem Seesteg)* of June 1916, Reprod. Cat. Feininger *Ged. Ausst.* 1961, No. 74.
6. Catalog, Feininger Memorial Exhib., Cleveland, 1961, No. 98.
7. Catalog, Feininger Memorial Exhib., Cleveland, 1961, No. 105.
8. Thomas Mann, "Germany and the Germans," *Yale Review,* XXXV, Dec. 1945, p. 223–41.
9. Charlotte Teller, *op. cit.*
10. Barr, p. 7.
11. The picture is reprod. in W. Wolfradt, *Lyonel Feininger,* in the series *Junge Kunst,* XLVII, Leipzig: 1924, and shows under the cycle of the Moon a Lake with three ships: a sailboat, a tug and a freighter. It was exhibited in the Feininger Show in the National Gallerie Berlin 1931, Catalog No. 64.
12. Barr, p. 11.
13. E. P. Richardson, *Painting in America,* New York: 1956, p. 377.
14. Letter of Paul Klee to Mme. Galka E. Scheyer, "How the title *The Blue Four* was chosen," in *The Blue Four,* Galka E. Scheyer Collection, Pasadena Art Museum.
15. "Mme. Scheyer Tells of Love for *Blue 4,*" by Inez Cunningham, *Chicago Evening Post,* Tuesday, April 12, 1932, on the occasion of *Blue 4* exhibit at the Renaissance Society of the University of Chicago.
16. Paintings by Feininger were included in the *Ausstellung Entartete Kunst,* München 1937. The catalog was published by the *Deutsche Reichs-Propagandaleitung,* Berlin."
17. Barr, *op. cit.,* p. 13.
18. Feininger met Mark Tobey in 1944. Though different in style, the two painters were spiritually very congenial, as we know from their exchange of letters, and from the "Comments by a Fellow Artist" by Lyonel and Julia Feininger, printed in the catalog entitled *Paintings by Mark Tobey,* Portland Art Museum, Portland: 1945. The two Feiningers wrote about Tobey's paintings that they reveal their tenor if one listens with the inner ear, "the ear of the heart" as the novelist Jean Paul Richter calls it, and they quote Tobey's words: "Light as a unifying idea leads through different stages of contemplation to tranquillity and peace," a statement characteristic also of Feininger and his development.

19. Examples in the possession of Mrs. Julia Feininger. The Busch-Reisinger Museum at Harvard University, Cambridge, Mass., owns pen and ink illustrations for an unpublished ghost story by Lyonel Feininger. This work is mentioned in Philip Hofer, *op. cit.*, p. 79.

20. Quoted in "Lyonel Feininger in Lincoln" by F. S. Wight, *op. cit.*, p. 10.

21. Barr, p. 13.

22. Lyonel Feininger: A memorial exhibition of his work from Fort Worth Collections March 6–April 1, 1956. Preface to the Catalog.

BIBLIOGRAPHY

Prefatory note:

The study *Lyonel Feininger, Caricature and Fantasy* is chiefly based on primary sources, that is, the letters written by the artist in English to two American friends of his youth and early manhood—H. Francis Kortheuer and Alfred Vance Churchill—and further on the two scrapbooks compiled by them.

Further information was obtained through an exchange of letters, personal interviews with members of the Feininger family, and with friends of the artist. Credit is given to them in the Acknowledgments; the character of these documents and the life of the recipients is further discussed in Chapter I.

A complete bibliography of the literature on Feininger, and the exhibitions of his work by Annemarie Heynig and Bernhard Karpel can be found together with the Oeuvre Catalog compiled by Mrs. Julia Feininger in Hans Hess, *Lyonel Feininger*, Kohlhammer Verlag, Stuttgart: 1959, the standard work on the subject.

Listed here are only those books and articles which are mentioned in the text and which have a direct or indirect bearing on the subject.

Ahlers-Hestermann, Friedrich, *Bruno Paul oder die Wucht des Komischen: 32 farbige Zeichnungen aus dem Simplicissimus,* Berlin: 1960.

Ahlers-Hestermann, Friedrich, "Der deutsche Künstlerkreis des Café du Dôme in Paris." *Kunst und Künstler.* XVI, Berlin, 1917–18.

Ahlers-Hestermann, Friedrich, *Pause vor dem dritten Akt.* Hamburg: 1949.

Barlach, Ernst, *Ein Selbsterzähltes Leben,* Berlin: 1921.

Barr, Alfred H. "Lyonel Feininger—American Artist," in *Lyonel Feininger—Marsden Hartley.* Exhibition, New York, Museum of Modern Art: 1944.

Busch, Wilhelm, *Max and Moritz,* edited and annotated by H. A. Klein, translated by H. A. Klein and others, New York: Dover, 1962.

Churchill, Alfred Vance, "Lyonel Feininger Woodcut Artist." *American Art Student.* VII, Jan. 1924.

Churchill, Alfred Vance, "Midwestern," *Northwestern Ohio Quarterly.* XIII, No. 1. (n.d.)

Cunningham, Inez, "Mme. Scheyer tells of love for 'Blue Four.'" *Chicago Evening Post,* April 12, 1932.

Däubler, Theodor, "Lyonel Feininger," *Das junge Deutschland,* Heft 10, Herausg (pub.). Deutsches Theater (Max Reinhardt), Berlin, 1919.

Feininger, Lyonel and Julia, "Comments by a Fellow Artist," Catalog, *Paintings by Mark Tobey. Portland Art Museum,* Portland: 1945.

Feininger, T. Lux, "Two Painters," *Chrysalis* IX, 9–10, Boston, 1956.

Grohmann, Will, *Karl Schmidt-Rottluff,* Stuttgart: 1956.

Grohmann, Will, *Wassily Kandinsky: Life and Work.* Translated from the German by Norbert Guterman. New York: 1958.

Hentzen, Alfred, *Lyonel Feininger,* Vorwort. Katalog. Gedächtnis Ausstellung 1871–1956. Museums Hamburg, Essen, Baden-Baden. 21. Jan. 26. Juni 1961.

Hermann, Georg, *Die Deutsche Karikatur im 19. Jahrhundert,* Bielefeld und Leipzig: 1901.

Hess, Hans, *Dank in Farben: Aus dem Gästebuch Alfred und Thekla Hess,* München: 1957.

Hess, Hans, *Lyonel Feininger,* Stuttgart: 1959.

Hess, Hans, *Lyonel Feininger,* London, Thames & Hudson: 1961. 650 illustrations, 28 color photos.

Hitchcock, Henry-Russell, "Alfred Vance Churchill," *75th Anniversary of Smith College,* Northampton, Mass., 1946.

Hofer, Philip, *The Artist and the Book 1860–1890,* Boston: 1961.

Liberman, Alexander, "In Feininger's Studio," *Vogue,* CXXVII, April 15, 1956.

Liebermann, William S., Introduction to *Lyonel Feininger, Kleine Blätter,* Catalog of an Exhibit, Berlin and Dortmund: 1962.

Louchheim, Aline, "Feininger looks back on 80 years," *New York Times,* March 23, 1952.

Mehring, Walter, *Verrufene Malerei: Von Malern, Kennern und Sammlern.* Zürich: 1958.

Moll, Margarete, "Erinnerungen an Henri Matisse," *Neue Deutsche Hefte.* Herausg. Paul Fechter und Joachim Günther. Feb. 23, 1956.

Murrell, William, *A History of American Graphic Humor.* Whitney Museum of American Art. New York: 1938.

Odell, C. D., *Annals of the New York Stage.* VIII–XII, Columbia University Press.

Peters, Harry T. *Currier and Ives. Print-makers to the American people.* New York: 1942.

Preetorius, Emil, *Lyonel Feininger.* Vorwort, Katalog der Ausstellung. München Bayerische Akademie der Künste. Sept.–Nov. 1954.

Rathbone, Perry T. *Lyonel Feininger Exhibition.* Preface. Detroit Institute of Arts—The Russell A. Alger House, Grosse Pointe, July–August 1941.

Richardson, Edgar Preston, *Painting in America: The Story of 450 Years,* New York: 1956.

Roth, Eugen, *Simplicissimus,* Hannover: 1954.

Ruhmer, Eberhard, *Lyonel Feininger Zeichnungen-Aquarelle-Graphik,* Munich: 1961.

Scheyer, Ernst, *Biedermeier in der Literatur und Kunstgeschichte,* Würzburg: 1960.

Scheyer, Ernst, *Die Breslauer Kunstakademie und Oskar Moll,* Würzburg: 1961.

Scheyer, Ernst, "Far Eastern Art and French Impressionism." *Art Quarterly,* Detroit: Spring 1943.

Scheyer, Ernst, "Japonism," *Encyclopedia of the Arts,* New York: 1946.

Schreyer, Lothar, *Lyonel Feininger, Dokumente und Visionen,* München: 1957.

Schreyer, Lothar, *Erinnerungen an Sturm und Bauhaus,* München: 1956.

Selz, Peter, *German Expressionist Painting.* Univ. of Calif.: 1957.

Soby, James Thrall, *Juan Gris.* Museum of Modern Art. New York: 1958.

Stein, Gertrude, *The Autobiography of Alice B. Toklas,* New York: 1933.

Teller, Charlotte, "Feininger Fantasist," *The International Studio,* LXIII, No. 249, New York: Nov. 1917.

Thormaehlen, Ludwig, *Lyonel Feininger,* Vorwort, Katalog der Ausstellung zum 60. Geburtstag, National Galerie, Berlin: 1931.

Tschudi, Hugo von, *Gesammelte Schriften zur Neueren Kunst.* München: 1912.

Wachtel, Joachim, *Lyonel Feininger, Karikaturen 1898–1910,* Introduction to a catalog of a travelling exhibit, 1963.

Werner, Alfred, *Jules Pascin,* New York: 1963.

Wight, Frederic S., "Feininger in Lincoln," Catalog Lyonel Feininger Exhibit. Cleveland Museum of Art, 1951.

Wolfradt, Willi, *Lyonel Feininger,* in *Junge Kunst.* XLVII, Leipzig: 1924.

Wolfradt, Willi, "Lyonel Feininger," *Jahrbuch der jungen Kunst,* Herausg. Georg Biermann. Leipzig: 1924.

INDEX

Abbey, Edwin Austin, 46, 60, 64, 179
Achenbach, Andreas, 51
Adams, Henry, 41
Ahlers-Hestermann, Friedrich, 101, 182, 183, 184
Albers, Joseph, 152
Ashbjornson, P., 184

Bach, Johann Sebastian, 13, 55, 84, 133, 134, 170
Bang, Hermann, 184
Bangs, John Kendrick, 59, 66
Barlach, Ernst, 24, 179
Barnum, P. T., 174
Barr, Alfred H., 19, 99, 125, 150, 154, 178, 179, 182, 184, 186
Beardsley, Aubrey, 94
Becher, J. R., 185
Beethoven, Ludwig von, 13
Berson, Arthur, 72, 181
Bing, S., 107
Bluemner, Rudolf, 139
Blum, Robert, 64
Böcklin, Arnold, 51
Bondy, Hans, 108
Bondy, Walter, 108
Brant, Cynthia, 154
Brant, Sebastian, 67
Braque, Georges, 131
Brooks, Charles T., 29
Bruegel, Pieter (the Elder), 83
Buffington, Leroy S., 16
Busch, Wilhelm, 20, 27, 28, 32, 66, 112, 180, 184
Buxtehude, Dietrich, 133, 170

Caspari, H., 94
Cézanne, Paul, 99, 100, 102, 127, 130, 154

Chamberlain, Joseph, 83
Chase, William, 24
Christopher, Francis, 145
Churchill, Alfred Vance, 8–9, 20, 29, 31, 32, 39, 40, 41, 43, 46, 48, 51, 53, 54, 55, 56, 58, 59, 62, 74, 79, 84, 94, 97, 124, 125–126, 127, 131, 132, 133, 134, 137, 139, 140, 141, 149, 150, 151, 157, 158, 164–165, 166–169, 170, 177, 179, 180, 182, 184, 185
Churchill, Marie, 140, 141, 170
Coburn, F., 53
Cooper, James Fenimore, 25, 173
Corinth, Lovis, 100, 132
Corot, Jean, 177
Crown Prince Friedrich, 69
Cruikshank, George, 30
Cunningham, Inez, 186
Currier, Nathaniel, 17

Damrosch, Leopold, 12, 178
Damrosch, Walter, 12, 178
Däubler, Theodor, 134, 139, 185
Dante, 56
de Fiori, Ernesto, 101
Delaunay, Elie, 128, 130, 167
Demuth, Charles, 150
Dickens, Charles, 25, 30, 173
Diez, Julius, 94
Dirk, Rudolf, 112
Doré, Gustav, 56, 180
Doyle, A. Conan, 25
Dreyer, Max, 108
Dreyfus, Alfred, 69, 164
Du Maurier, George, 25

Eisner, Kurt, 185
Engel, F., 70
Eysler, Dr., 68, 81

Feininger, Alois Adolph Michael, 11
Feininger, Andreas, 8
Feininger, Elizabeth Lutz, 12, 172, 174
Feininger, Elsa, 16, 171, 172, 174
Feininger, Gabrielle, 12
Feininger, Helen, 16, 171, 172
Feininger, Julia, 8, 15, 51, 60, 64, 97, 98, 100, 114, 123, 130, 145, 170, 175, 178, 184, 186, 187
Feininger, Karl Friedrich Wilhelm, 11–13, 18, 40, 166, 171, 172
Feininger, Laurence, 8, 77
Feininger, Lena Brennioni, 11
Feininger, Theodore Lux, 8, 17, 68, 124, 129, 178, 181, 184
Friedrich, Caspar David, 96
Friedrich, Crown Prince, 69
Friedrich, Woldemar, 53, 54, 180
Friesz, Othon, 128, 167
Frost, A. B., 64, 66, 180
Fulda, Max, 89

Gauguin, Paul, 99, 102, 127, 134
Géricault, Theodore, 177
Gehrke, Fritz, 70
Gerlach, Martin, 109
Gibson, Charles Dana, 64
Gleizes, Albert, 130
Goethe, Johann Wolfgang von, 180
Goetz, Richard, 130, 184
Gris, Juan, 106–7, 130, 181, 183
Grohmann, W., 182, 185
Gropius, Walter, 140, 152
Grossmann, Rudolf, 99, 101, 102
Gruenicke, Franz, 180

Hamid, Abdul, 81
Hancke, Ernst, 49, 53, 160, 179
Harte, Bret, 25, 54, 55, 56
Hartley, Marsden, 150, 152
Hasenclever, Walter, 185
Hauptmann, Gerhart, 89
Hearst, William Randolph, 112
Heckel, Erich, 132
Heilemann, Ernst, 86
Heine, Thomas Theodor, 86, 94

Hentzen, Alfred, 147, 184
Hermann, Georg, 85, 89, 93, 94, 181, 182
Herriman, George, 122
Hess, Hans, 86, 120, 145, 147, 178–186 *passim*
Hessel, Franz, 101
Hildebrandt, Eduard, 51
Hitchcock, Henry Russell, 178
Hitler, Adolf, 149
Hofer, Philip, 184, 187
Hoffmann, E. T. A., 143, 149
Hohenlohe-Schillingsfürst, Chlodwig von, 79
Hokusai, 109
Howard, Catherine, 103
Howard, Wilhelm, 103

Iribe, Paul, 93, 103, 106, 107
Ives, James, 17

Jawlensky, Alexei von, 151
Jenney, William Le Baron, 16
Johnson, Ch. H., 64

Kahnweiler, D. H., 183
Kandinsky, Wassily, 95, 96, 150, 182
Keeley, James, 111, 114
Keppler, Joseph, 34
Kipling, Rudyard, 25
Klee, Paul, 146, 151, 186
Klein, H. Arthur, 184
Kloth (Professor), 41
Knoblauch, Adolf, 16, 139, 149, 185
Kokoschka, Oskar, 109
Kortheuer, Arthur, 164, 171
Kortheuer, Dayrell, 157
Kortheuer, Florence Marshall, 171
Kortheuer, Hermann O. C., 171
Kortheuer, H. Francis, 8–9, 10, 18, 20–21, 22, 23, 24, 25, 26, 28, 29, 30, 31, 35, 36, 39, 48, 49, 60, 62, 63, 64, 66, 69, 70, 72, 74, 78, 84, 86, 97, 98, 125, 149, 151, 157, 162, 171, 176–78, 180, 181, 182
Kortheuer, Teresa, 162

Kramer, Eduard A., 125, 164
Krüger, Franz, 53
Kubin, Alfred, 132, 145

La Farge, John, 47
Larkin, Oliver W., 179
Le Fauconnier, Henri, 128, 130, 167
Leger, Ferdinand, 130
Lehmbruck, Wilhelm, 101
Leistikow, Walter, 100
Levy, Rudolf, 99, 100, 101, 102
L'Hermitte, Léon, 58, 59, 160
Liberman, Alexander, 178
Liebermann, Max, 98, 101, 132
Lincoln, Abraham, 94
Louchheim, Aline, 123, 184
Lucas, E. V., 179

Macke, August, 130
Makart, Hans, 51
Manet, Edouard, 101
Mann, Thomas, 95, 96, 149, 182, 186
Manzel, Ludwig, 70
Marc, Franz, 130, 132
Marin, John, 150
Marshall, Hilda, 24, 27, 164, 171, 172
Marshall, Marie, 9
Martin, E. S., 34
Matisse, Henri, 98, 99, 100, 101, 131, 184
Maurer, Louis, 178
Mehring, Siegmar, 69, 70
Mehring, Walter, 70, 181
Meidner, Ludwig, 185
Meier-Graefe, Julius, 107, 182
Meitzner, Herr Regierungsrat, 29
Mendelssohn, Felix, 11, 13
Menzel, Adolf von, 49, 53
Metzinger, Jean, 130
Miquel, Johann von, 77, 79
Mitchell, J. A., 34
Moe, J., 184
Moll, Margarete, 98, 99, 124
Moll, Oskar, 98, 99, 100
Monet, Claude, 58, 98, 160
Mueller, Felix, 132, 185
Murrell, William, 179, 180

Napoleon I, 59
Newell, Peter, 64, 66
Nolde, Emil, 104

Oberländer, Adolf, 64, 72, 180
Odell, C. D., 178
Opper, Frederick Burr, 64, 180
Outcault, Richard F., 35, 122

Paganini, Nicolò, 12
Pascin, Jules, 99, 102, 131, 145
Paul, Bruno, 86, 182
Pechstein, Max, 132, 185
Pennell, Joseph, 46, 48, 179
Peters, Harry T., 178
Picasso, Pablo, 102, 106, 128, 131, 167
Piloty, Karl Theodor von, 180
Prasse, Leona F., 186
Prealle, J., 23, 27
Preetorius, Emil, 72
Prince of Wales, 83
Pulitzer, Joseph, 35
Purrmann, Hans, 99, 100, 101, 183
Pyle, Howard, 64

Ramberg, Arthur Georg, 180
Rathbone, Perry T., 178, 184
Rathenau, Walter, 178
Reinhardt, C. J., 64
Reis, B. J. (Mr. and Mrs.), 183
Rembrandt, 159
Richardson, E. P., 150
Richter, Jean Paul, 186
Richter, Ludwig, 62
Riou, Edouard, 57, 180
Roebling, John A., 15
Roebling, Washington, 15
Roosevelt, Theodore, 84
Roth, Eugen, 182
Ruhmer, Eberhard, 183

St. Lucas, 32
Sauerbronn, Baron Karl Drais von, 16
Schardt, A., 185
Scheyer, Ernst, 171, 182, 184
Scheyer, Galka E., 151, 185, 186

Schlabitz, Adolph, 49, 179
Schmidt-Cabanis, R., 70
Schmidt-Rottluff, Karl, 132
Schoenleber, Gustav, 51
Schreyer, Lothar, 132, 139, 148, 178, 185
Schubert, Franz, 13
Schumann, Robert, 13
Schurz, Carl, 11
Schwartzman, Adolph, 34
Scott, Walter, 180
Selz, Peter, 98, 100, 124, 132, 183, 185
Shakespeare, William, 179
Smedley, W. T., 64
Snyder, W. P., 178
Soby, James Thrall, 107, 183
Spitzweg, Karl, 96
Sprengel, Bernhard, 181
Steffeck, Karl, 53, 180
Stein, Gertrude, 101, 183
Steiner-Prag, Hugo, 109
Stephan, Postmaster, 79
Stevenson, Robert Louis, 25
Strothmann, Frederick, 174, 175
Stöcker, Adolf, 79
Sudermann, Heinrich, 89
Suering, Reinhard, 181

Teller, Charlotte, 21, 131, 150, 178, 179, 184, 186
Thormaehlen, Ludwig, 133, 182
Thorvaldsen, Barthel, 24
Tiffany, Louis Comfort, 47, 48

Titian, 159
Tobey, Mark, 152, 186
Tschudi, Hugo von, 182
Turner, J. M. W., 8, 18, 39, 46
Twain, Mark, 101

Uhde, Wilhelm, 101

Valentiner, W. R., 184
Vanderbilt, Commodore, 14
Van Gogh, Vincent, 99, 127, 134, 167, 168
Verne, Jules, 57, 173, 180
Villon, Jacques, 152
Vogel, Hermann, 60, 62

Wachtel, Joachim, 181
Walden, Herwarth, 132, 139, 146, 185
Weisgerber, Leo, 101
Werner, Alfred, 183
Werner, Fred, 40, 54, 55, 56, 180
Westheim, Paul, 185
Whistler, James, 5, 46, 48, 130
Whitman, Walter, 14
Wight, Frederic S., 178, 179, 187
Wilhelmi, August D. F. von, 11
Wilke, Rudolf, 86
Woldemar (The Dane), 24
Wolfradt, Willy, 96, 178, 182

Zech, Paul, 185
Zimmerman, Eugene (Zim), 29, 30, 31, 64

The manuscript was edited by Richard Dey. The book was designed by Richard Kinney. The type face for the text is Linotype Caledonia designed by W. A. Dwiggins in 1940. The display is Venus Extra Bold Extended cut for Bauer, 1907–13.

The book is printed on S. D. Warren's Patina paper and bound in Joanna Mills, Beaverbrook cloth over boards. Manufactured in the United States of America.